Transform Your
HOME
in a weekend

Transform Your
HOME
in a weekend

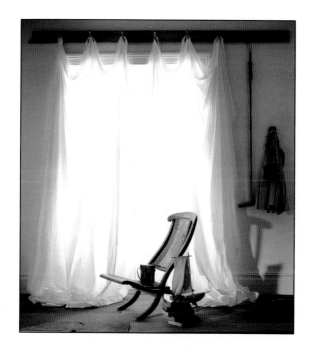

Stewart & Sally Walton

SELECT
EDITIONS

Select Editions imprint specially produced for Selectabook Ltd.

Produced by Anness Publishing Limited
Hermes House, 88–89 Blackfriars Road, London SE1 8HA

ISBN 1-84081-128-5

A CIP catalogue record for this book is available from the British Library

Publisher: Joanna Lorenz
Senior editors: Lindsay Porter, Clare Nicholson
Photographer: Graham Rae
Stylists: Catherine Tully, Judy Smith, Andrea Spencer, Diana Civil
Designer: Simon Wilder

Also published as *Instant Decorating*

Printed and bound in Hong Kong

© Anness Publishing Limited 1997, 1999
1 3 5 7 9 10 8 6 4 2

CONTENTS

WINDOWS 6

WALLS AND FLOORS 54

BEDS AND BEDDING 92

CHAIRS AND TABLES 130

LIGHT AND SHADE 168

CONTAINERS 212

INDEX 254

WINDOWS

Egyptian Dream ♦ Curtain Call ♦ White Mischief ♦ Shell Tie-Backs

Crystal Ties ♦ Bijou Boudoir ♦ Rainbows ♦ No-Problem Links

Ribbons and Lace ♦ Wired-Up Window ♦ African Days

Robinson Crusoe Blinds ♦ Artist's Studio ♦ Buttoned Blankets ♦ Hula-Hula

Scotland the Brave ♦ Magic Beads ♦ Mad Hatter ♦ Hanging Around

$\mathscr{I}$NTRODUCTION

Above: There is no need to hide blankets away in the bedroom; here, they have been transformed into a rich and colourful window treatment which perfectly complements the simple furnishings in this living room.

BASEMENT, BALCONY, OR BEDSIT - whatever the style of your home and whatever you're looking to achieve, you're certain to find something here to revolutionize your windows. So, if you thought it was all just plastic curtain hooks and tracks, read on! All you have to do is invest in a staple gun and some inexpensive fittings and fixings, and follow our simple step-by-step instructions to show you exactly how to make your windows the fabulous focal point of each room. You will never look in curtain departments again once you have been shown our instant window makeovers and realize how easy it is to create stunning and dramatic effects. The ideas in this book will carry you away from traditional methods and old-fashioned styles towards the freshness and freedom of experimental window dressing. Many of our projects were inspired by looking at familiar materials in a new light, such as using grass beach mats for blinds or tartan wool rugs for an imposing curtain. There are all kinds of materials that can make the leap from their everyday practical uses to highly original ones. This chapter contains projects to suit every taste and every budget including quick stylish ideas for tie-backs, hanging treatments and colour schemes and simple effects created by draping, typing, stapling, buttoning, hanging, clipping and glueing all kinds of fabrics. You will probably come up with your own ideas and variations on our themes, too. So, armed with this innovative book, take a fresh look at the windows around your home and have lots of fun transforming them to reflect your personality. The real beauty of our quick and inexpensive window dressing ideas is that, if you happen to change your mind at a later date, you can simply come up with another one!

Below left: A blank canvas becomes a work of art in this imposing project, which is ideally suited to a room with a high ceiling.

Below right: Transparent beads sparkle like jewels in the light from even a small window. As well as adding brightness, the tall shape of the bead curtain helps to elongate the natural focal point of the room.

EGYPTIAN DREAM

A PAIR OF COTTON SHEETS makes the most wonderful drape and all the seams are perfectly finished. The bigger the sheets, the more luxurious and elegant the window will look – drapes should always be generous.

Wooden pegs can be wedged into a piece of old wooden floorboarding or driftwood – if you drill the holes at an angle, the fixing will be stronger as well as more decorative.

YOU WILL NEED

scissors

cotton tape, 2.5 m
(2½ yd)

2 flat king-size cotton sheets

needle and white sewing
thread

drill

length of floorboarding or
driftwood, window width
plus 15cm (6in) either side

6 old-fashioned wooden pegs

spirit level

wallplugs and screws

screwdriver

one *With scissors, cut the cotton tape into six strips of equal length.*

two *Divide the width of each sheet top by three and use the divisions as points to attach the tapes. Fold each tape in half and use small stitches to sew them to the top of the sheet.*

three *Drill six holes at equal distances along the floorboarding and wedge in the pegs. Drill a hole either end of the floorboarding and screw it into the wall, using a spirit level to check it is straight, and appropriate fixings to secure it.*

four *Tie the tapes securely and neatly to the pegs and arrange the drapes.*

CURTAIN CALL

THIS IS AN EXTREMELY QUICK and effective way to trim the top edge of a loop-headed curtain. Tie ribbons round the loops and hang a selection of beautiful decorations from them. Here we have used pieces of pot-pourri but you could also use odd earrings, bells, tin stars, buttons and so on. If you have a pinch-pleated or a simple gathered curtain heading, a small bow or knot with ribbon hanging down would look effective.

YOU WILL NEED

tape measure

1cm (½in) wide hessian or linen

ribbon or tape

dressmaker's scissors

needle and matching sewing thread (optional)

pot-pourri

glue gun and glue sticks

one *Decide the appropriate length or lengths of ribbon or tape needed in relation to the drop of the curtain, so that they look in proportion.*

two *Cut the ribbon or tape to length and cut the ends at an angle, so they look neat. If you are using a ribbon that frays, hem the ends. Select the pieces of pot-pourri that most complement one another. Using a glue gun, attach the pieces of pot-pourri to the ends of the ribbon or tape.*

three *Tie the ribbon or tape to the curtain loops. It is best not to fix them permanently, so you can change the design when you wish and take them off when you wash the curtains.*

WHITE MISCHIEF

SMALL DETAILS SUCH AS the curtain clips in this project make the important difference between an obvious and an elegant solution to curtain hanging. The white muslin lawn is a generously long piece, folded in half, allowing a drop 1½ times the length of the window – it really is a very simple, yet elegant example of window dressing! Small brass curtain clips fit over the rail and catch the muslin along the fold.

YOU WILL NEED

dowel, window width

woodstain

kitchen cloth

drill

wallplugs and nails

hammer

curtain clips

white muslin lawn

wooden spear or a garden implement

one *Stain the length of dowel by shaking woodstain on to a soft cloth and rubbing the dowel with it until you achieve the effect you want.*

two *Drill two holes either side of the window in the wall and insert the wallplugs. Bang in the nails.*

three *Clip the muslin along the fold, leaving an equal distance between the clips. Thread the rings on to the dowel and place the dowel over the nails.*

four *Spread the rings along the dowel so that the muslin falls in even drapes.*

five *Knot the front drop of muslin on to the end of the spear and prop this across the window.*

SHELL TIE-BACKS

CURTAIN TIE-BACKS can be made in a tremendously wide range of styles so you can use them to create whatever decorative effect you like. Though we normally think of a simple braid or tassel, tie-backs can be trimmed to make them focal- and talking-points within the room. Here a fishing net was festooned with different types and sizes of shells. You could wire a mass of very small shells on to the net or even edge the curtain with a widely spaced line of matching shells.

YOU WILL NEED
fishing net

shells

fine wire

wire cutters

glue gun and glue sticks
or electric drill, with very
fine drill bit

string (optional)

one *Take the fishing net and arrange it in graceful folds. Gather together a mass of shells and see how they look best when arranged on the net.*

Cut lengths of fine wire. These can then be glued to the back of the shells so that they can be wired on to the netting.

two *Alternatively, drill holes in the shells. Thread string through the holes for attaching to the net.*

three *Fix the shells on the netting. Make another tie-back in the same way. Loop the tie-backs around the curtains and on to the wall.*

CRYSTAL TIES

TIE AN EXQUISITE SILK curtain with crystal drops for an elegant look. The use of a very rough hessian tassel, bound quite casually and loosely, makes this interesting and unusual. The crystal drops were bought from an antique shop; search around for interesting examples. Failing that, use crystal drops from a bead shop or coloured stones from a cheap necklace or earrings, all of which will look equally lovely.

YOU WILL NEED

hessian tassel tie-back
scissors
crystal chandelier drops
gold beading wire or very
fine gold string
wire cutters

one *You need only one tassel tie-back for two curtains. Split the tassel in half, then unravel the rope. Re-bind the tassel to make it look less formal.*

two *Thread the crystal drops on to gold wire or fine string to make several lengths of various sizes.*

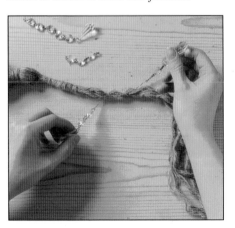

three *Fasten the lengths of crystal drops on to the tie-backs. Some will simply hook on; others should be wired. Loop the tie-backs around the curtains and on to the wall.*

$\mathscr{B}$IJOU BOUDOIR

BALLROOM DANCERS, bad-taste rockers, brides and prima ballerinas all love it – netting has that special star quality that windows sometimes need! You can cut, pleat, layer, scrunch and bunch it – there is nothing to sew and it is so light that many filmy, glamorous lengths can hang from a single strand of plastic-coated sprung wire.

Netting comes in all sorts of colours and the idea from this project could easily be translated into a completely stunning party window in dramatic purple or scarlet and black. Tie the the lengths of netting back with feather boas, strings of pearls or even kitsch diamanté dog collars to make the most glamorous window this side of Cannes.

YOU WILL NEED

pliers

4 eyelet hooks

2 lengths of plastic-coated
sprung wire,
window width

4 m (4 yd) each pink and
white netting

scissors

fine wire

feather boa

fake pearl strands

one *Screw in an eyelet hook at the same height either side of the window recess.*

two *Loop the eyelet on the wire through the hooks and stretch the wire taut across the window.*

three *Repeat the process, positioning the second wire about 8cm (3in) in front of the first (of course, this distance will be dictated by the depth of your window recess).*

four *Cut the netting in half. Feed half the length of the pink netting over the back wire. Set aside the rest of the pink netting.*

five *Feed the length of the white netting over the back wire, next to the pink netting. Pull both lengths of netting into shape, making a double layer with each.*

six *Hang the other layer of pink netting over the front wire.*

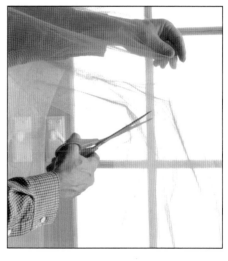

seven *Cut out a large circle of pink netting to make the pelmet and fold this over the front wire to create a semi-circle.*

eight *Cut long strips of netting and scrunch them into rosettes. Tuck them between the wires. You will find that the netting is very easy to scrunch into good shapes. Pleat up the semi-circular pelmet, adding folds and creases along the wire as you go.*

CONTINUED OVER ➤

nine *Make big white rosettes to go into the corners by scrunching up the white netting. Tuck them into the wire to secure and smooth them out to make a pleasing shape.*

ten *Twist the fine wire into connecting rings and use them to attach the feather boa along the curve of the netting pelmet.*

eleven *Drape the strands of fake pearls from the centre of the front wire and tie up the ends.*

Right: One of the great advantages of netting is that it is easy to handle, and is quite forgiving. If you don't like the first shape you have made, smooth it out and scrunch it up again. These rosettes are simply tucked between the front and back.

RAINBOWS

THIS REALLY MUST BE THE QUICKEST, cheapest and brightest way to deal with a bare kitchen window. It would also work well in a hall or on a small staircase window. All you need to do is buy an insect blind – those door-length, multi-coloured plastic strips. Then screw two cup hooks into the window frame to hold the rail and get your scissors out for a trim! The one in this project is V-shaped, but zig-zags, rippling waves, castellations or even asymmetrical designs are equally possible.

YOU WILL NEED
ruler
pencil
wooden rail
2 cup hooks
door-size insect blind
scissors

one *Place the rail along the top of the window and position the cup hooks so that the strips will hang over the whole width of the window.*

two *Measure the windowsill to find the mid-point and make a small mark. This is where the blind will touch.*

three *Place the ruler on a slant between the mark and the point you want the side drop to reach. Measure and mark the same point on the other side of the window frame.*

four *Hang the insect blind on the rail and position it on the hooks, then hold the ruler up against it, between the two pencil marks. Cut the strips along the top of the ruler.*

No-PROBLEM LINKS

WHAT LENGTHS WILL YOU GO TO for a bargain? If you find the fabric of your dreams in the remnant bin, but it's just that bit too short for your window, it's no longer a problem. Use curtain rings to connect the different lengths of fabric you have found – you can use as many as you need for the drop. Nobody will ever suspect that the linked effect was anything other than a deliberate design decision.

YOU WILL NEED

drill

spirit level

wallplugs and screws

screwdriver

metal curtain rail and fixings

assorted lengths of remnant fabrics

iron-on hem fix
(such as Wundaweb)

iron

needle and matching sewing thread

split curtain rings

one *Attach the rail fixings above the window. Check with a spirit level before you screw them to the wall. Assemble the curtain rail and fixings.*

two *Hem all the rough edges of the fabric, either with iron-on hem fix or by hand. Sew small split rings along the top edge of the curtain to link into the rail rings. Sew rings in the same positions along the bottom of the first piece of fabric.*

three *Line the curtain up with the next piece of fabric and mark the positions for attaching the rings. Make sure they line up exactly with the first curtain if you have a geometric or striped pattern. Sew the rings to the second piece of fabric along the whole width, then hang in place.*

Above: The curtains can be linked with single rings, split rings or interconnecting rings like these.

RIBBONS AND LACE

MAKE THE MOST OF A BEAUTIFUL PIECE of sari fabric or a superb lace panel by displaying it in a window so that the light shines through. A few hand-stitched lengths of ribbon will allow you to tie back the fabric to reveal as much or as little of the window and the view as you like.

As the main fabric is very light and translucent, hang a length of white muslin behind it for extra privacy.

YOU WILL NEED

muslin, 1½ x window width

iron-on hem fix
(such as Wundaweb)

iron

white tape

thread

dowel, window width

2 cup hooks

scissors

white or cream linen or
satin ribbon

sari fabric or antique
lace panel

one *Finish the hems on the muslin with iron-on hem fix, then sew lengths of white tape along the top to tie the muslin to the dowel. Screw the hooks into the window frame and hang up the dowel rail. Tie the curtain on to the rail.*

two *Cut the ribbon into eight 25cm (10in) lengths and stitch four along the top edge of the sari fabric or lace panel. Stitch the others at intervals along the sides – their positions will depend on the size of the panel and the parts that you want to show off. You can also hide any defects when you tie them up in this way.*

three *Tie the top ribbons to the rail using simple bows. Arrange them along the rail so that the fabric drapes over the window in the most appealing way.*

four *Tie up sections of the panel using the side ribbons. Experiment with different combinations, standing back from the window to check your adjustments until you are happy.*

WIRED-UP WINDOW

THIS IS A QUIRKY PROJECT for people who see the window as a frame to be filled, but not necessarily frilled! A selection of crisp Irish linen tea towels, linen scrim window cloths, dusters and oven gloves are arranged on a wire framework of tracks and hangers for a practical and stylish window treatment in the kitchen. Yachting chandlers sell good wire with all kinds of interesting bits and pieces for fastening and tightening up. Follow the steps here for an explanation on how to use them and to ensure everything connects securely.

Look at this window treatment as a moveable feast and re-position the key elements every now and again for a new design at no extra cost.

YOU WILL NEED

rigging wire, 2 x window width; 1 x ½ window length, plus 30cm (12in)

fixed rigging wire grips and thimbles

adjustable rigging wire grips and thimbles

hammer

pliers

2 deck eyes with pulleys

2 fixed deck eyes

bradawl

rigging screw (tension adjuster)

connecting rings (key-ring style), various sizes

wire coat hangers

selection of tea towels, dusters, and oven gloves

one *To make the rigging, thread the rigging wire through the fixed wire grip to form a loop with the end.*

two *Place the thimble inside the loop and pull the wire tight, so it fits snugly round the thimble. Place it on a hard surface and bang the wire grip closed with a hammer.*

three *Loosen the screw on the adjustable wire grip and thimble and thread the other end of the wire through. Tighten the screw to hold the wire firmly in place.*

four *Cut off the excess wire at the point where it enters the thimble.*

five *Loop the thimble fitting over a deck eye, then hold it in position to the window frame while you use a bradawl to make holes for the screws. Screw the deck eye securely into the window frame.*

six *Thread the wire through one of the pulleys and screw this pulley into the window frame opposite the first fixing.*

seven *Thread the wire through the second pulley and screw this pulley into the window frame halfway down the side of the window.*

eight *Attach a thimble to the end of the shorter length of wire. Loop this through a deck eye and screw it into the frame halfway down the side of the window – opposite the last pulley.*

CONTINUED OVER ➤

nine *Attach an adjustable wire grip so that it can join on to each end of the rigging screw. Because of the nature of a rigging screw, you will be able to make minor adjustments to centralize it, but aim to cut the wire as accurately as possible to begin with. Twist the rigging screw to increase the tension.*

ten *To assemble the arrangement, use connecting rings to link the wire coat hangers together.*

eleven *You could also make up 'cat's cradle' shapes by interlinking hangers. Always reinforce the links with rings to make them more secure.*

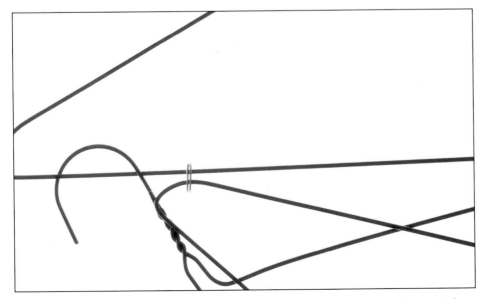

twelve *To make further variations of the linked coat hangers, experiment with them until you are pleased with the arrangement.*

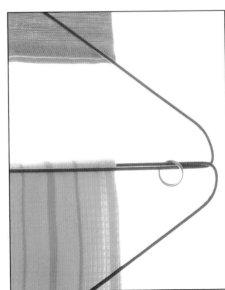

thirteen *Finally, iron the tea towels and fold them over the hangers.*

AFRICAN DAYS

KENYAN CLOTHS ARE GORGEOUSLY rich and vibrant. The patterns and colours are bold and brilliant and there is no need to hem, stitch or gather them. Just run a washing line across the window and peg the cloth on to it – use colour co-ordinated clothes pegs and line to pull this easy and exotic window treatment together.

You won't be able to draw this curtain, but keep an extra peg or two handy so you can use them to hold the cloth back and let the sunshine in – even on a rainy day!

YOU WILL NEED

2 cup hooks or eyelets
plastic-coated washing line
multi-coloured plastic pegs
African cloth panel

one *Screw the hooks into the wall (or window frame) at an equal distance from the window.*

two *Loop the washing line around the hooks and tie a knot.*

three *Peg the cloth to the line, gathering it up a bit for the first and last pegs to add weight around the edges.*

four *Bundle up the excess line on one side and tie it in a knot. Let this hang down instead of cutting it off.*

ROBINSON CRUSOE BLINDS

THIS REALLY MUST BE one of the cheapest, simplest, yet most effective blind solutions ever: it involves two grass beach mats, three cup hooks, a length of rope and some brass paper fasteners. The beach mats are made with coloured tape binding, and as they are extremely light-weight, they can be rolled up by hand and tied with rope.

Measure your window carefully – the mats are available in one width only, so they are not suitable for all types and sizes of window.

YOU WILL NEED
bradawl
3 cup hooks
2 grass beach mats
paper fasteners
rope
scissors

one *Make three holes with a bradawl, one either side and one in the middle of the window recess. Screw in the cup hooks.*

two *Make a channel for the rope at the top of the blind by folding over the mat 4cm (1½in) and securing with a row of evenly spaced paper fasteners, pushed through and folded back.*

three *Knot the rope on to one of the cup hooks, leaving a tail hanging about a third of the way down the window. Thread the rope through the blind and pull it tight before knotting it on to the middle hook. Cut the rope the same length as before.*

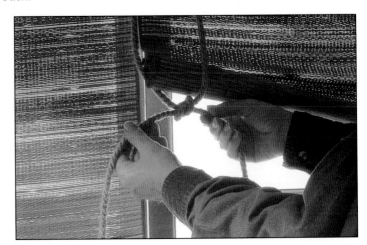

four *Cut a length of rope twice the length of the window drop and knot it in the middle, on to the middle hook. Roll up the blind by hand and tie the two ends of this rope to hold it at the required height. Repeat this process with a second length of rope for the second blind.*

ARTIST'S STUDIO

THIS IS THE IDEAL WAY to cover a large studio window, and as canvas comes in so many sizes, you're bound to find a piece to fit your window. If you have never previously considered the possibility of becoming a painter, then this is a good way to start – curtains can also be art!

Here, chalks were used to draw on to the canvas and change the flat panel into a boldly gathered backdrop. You could use this idea as your inspiration, or you could flick colours on it in Jackson Pollock style, or simply add a few minimalist squiggles. If your window receives a lot of light, you may want to suspend a builder's dust-sheet in front of the window. This will provide a lining for the main curtain.

YOU WILL NEED

canvas, 1½ x window width

chalks or acrylic paints and paintbrush

drill

4 chunky garage hooks

screwdriver

metal cleat

rope

double-sided carpet tape

brass eyelets

hammer

one *Draw, paint or print on to the canvas using whatever style or design you have chosen – the bolder the better, as the canvas will cover a large surface area.*

two *Fix the garage hooks securely into the wall above the window, spaced at equal intervals.*

three *Screw the cleat to the wall, about halfway down the side of the window, then wind one end of the rope around it several times.*

four *Take the long end of the rope up and through the hooks along the top.*

five *Pull the rope taut and tie it on to the end hook. Then fix the seams and eyelets on to the canvas following the manufacturer's instructions.*

six *Thread the rope through the first eyelet from behind, allowing about 16cm (6¼in) between the hook and the eyelet. Then, leaving the same distance again, twist a loop in the rope and put it on the hook.*

seven *Take the rope down and through the back of the next eyelet, then up and over the back taut rope, which now forms a 'rail' for the rope to rest on.*

eight *When you reach the end of the curtain, take the rope through the last hook.*

nine *Take the rope straight down the side of the window and tie it neatly on to the cleat.*

ten Cut an extra length of rope and hook it over one of the top centre hooks so that one length falls to the front and the other to the back of the canvas. Gather the canvas up and get hold of both ends of the rope. Tie these together in a knot and leave the ends dangling free.

Above: The knot holding the curtain back from the window allows the light to come through.

Above: Allow plenty of canvas so that it spills generously out on to the floor below the window.

Above: The knotted rope forms an additional decorative element in its own right.

Above: The natural colour of the canvas enhances the subtle colours of the design.

BUTTONED BLANKETS

THESE BLANKETS WERE too brilliant to hide away in the bedroom so they were transformed into an attractive window treatment. They make good draught excluders and are simply rigged up on a couple of towel rails. You need a solid wall as the blankets are weighty. The blankets are doubled over and held together with a row of large safety pins.

YOU WILL NEED

2 chrome towel rails

drill

wallplugs and extra-long screws

screwdriver

2 colourful wool blankets

10 large coloured buttons, to contrast with blanket colours

dressmaker's pins or double-sided tape

large safety pins or nappy pins

tailors' chalk

needle and button thread or wool

one *Fix the towel rails to the wall above the window, by drilling holes and inserting wallplugs. As towel rails are not long enough to cover the whole width, hang them at different heights.*

two *Fold both the blankets in half lengthways. Drape them over the curtain rails, to create a 30cm (12in) pelmet as shown. Take down the blankets. Decide upon the position of the buttons, trying them out by fixing them to the blankets with dressmaker's pins or with double-sided tape.*

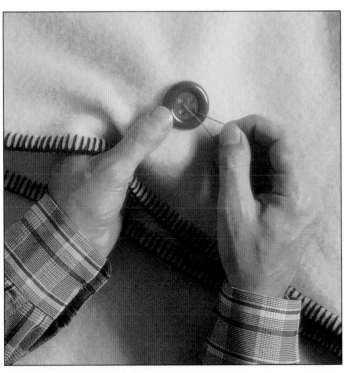

three *Stitch the buttons along the pelmet, just catching the first layer with a few stitches to secure the buttons, but without damaging the blanket.*

four *Pin a row of safety pins about halfway down the pelmet, on the underside where they won't show. Hang the blankets back in position. Re-pin carefully, so that each safety pin goes through the inside layer of the pelmet, and the outer layer of the curtain.*

Hula-Hula

ORDINARY WINDBREAKS used on the beach can be transformed into instant blinds. They come in a range of lengths with poles in pockets to divide the equal sections, just like a Roman blind, but bolder. All you have to do is saw off the extra piece of pole that goes into the sand and hang up the blind on a couple of plumbers' pipe fittings. A wide range of cheerful summer colours is available.

YOU WILL NEED
windbreak, to fit window

scissors

stapler

saw

tape measure

drill

2 wallplugs

2 plumbers' pipe fittings

screwdriver

flower garlands, elastic or rope

string (optional)

one *Hold the windbreak vertically against your window. If the drop is too long, then cut out the nylon mesh and make a new channel for the bottom pole. Fold over a hem, making sure the pole fits, and staple along the edge.*

two *Saw off the excess pole, then measure the window and the top of the blind to find the position for the fixings. Drill holes and insert the wallplugs and plumbers' fittings.*

three *Hang the blind, then loop the garlands, elastic or rope between the first and last poles. If the garlands are too long, tie them in divisions with string to shorten.*

SCOTLAND THE BRAVE

HERE IS THE PERFECT WAY to show off bright tartan wool rugs. Draped and pinned over a wooden rail, they will add a baronial touch to the plainest of windows.

Tartan has quite a masculine feel and looks good alongside old leather cases and other "practical" accessories. This window would suit a study or hallway with plain walls, contrasting with the richness and pattern of the tartan. Fix the curtain rail above the window, extending about 30cm (12in) each side.

YOU WILL NEED

wooden curtain rail

spirit level

drill

wallplugs and screws

screwdriver

3 different coloured tartan rugs

6 kilt pins

one *Fix the curtain rail according to the pack instructions. Begin on the left with one corner of a rug. Take the corner over from the back and pin it about 30cm (12in) down the rug.*

two *Drape the second rug over the rail, also on the left, but arrange it so that the drape is more or less equal at the front and back. Lift it in places and pin it on to the first rug using kilt pins.*

three *Drape the third tartan rug along the rest of the pole diagonally so that the fringed edge can be seen hanging down from the right corner. Lift sections of this rug and pin it in drapes by attaching it with kilt pins to the second rug.*

four *Stand back and check the effect, then use any remaining pins to hold the rugs in place, making a feature of the fringing and the pins.*

MAGIC BEADS

TRANSPARENT BEADS DON'T block out the light or keep out the draughts, but when the sun catches them, they sparkle like jewels, and using them full-length on a small square window can turn a light source into something bright and magical. Beads are available in brilliant, gem-like colours, softly co-ordinated pastels and clear colourless textures and each has its own unique, light-enhancing quality.

YOU WILL NEED

2 wooden battens, window width, plus 8–10cm (3–4in) each side

wood glue

hammer

panel pins

ruler

emulsion paint: black and white

paintbrush

drill

coloured bead curtain, with fixing strip and screws

screwdriver

wallplugs and screws

spirit level

small jewelled drawer knob

one *Make the pelmet by sticking one edge of a batten to the long edge of the other to form a right angle. Hammer in a few panel pins to secure it. Divide the length into equal sections and paint them alternately black and white.*

two *Drill, then screw through the holes in the bead fixing strip to secure it underneath the pelmet.*

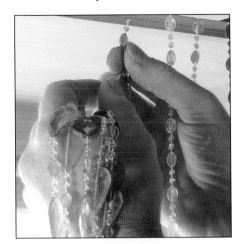

three *Drill, insert wallplugs and screw the pelmet in place above the window. Use a spirit level to check the position after attaching one side. Hang the lengths of beads, in a pattern or at random, along the fixing strip.*

four *Drill a hole, insert a wallplug and screw in the drawer knob in position – level with the base of the window if it is a small one, or halfway down if you have got a larger window.*

MAD HATTER

IF YOU HAVE EVER felt like going right over the top with your home decorating, milliner's velvet must be the curtain choice for you! Milliner's velvet comes in gorgeous colours and it is great to work with. It is backed with paper and folds into the biggest cabbage roses and most luscious drapes imaginable. A window treatment such as this is definitely not for those of a shy and retiring disposition!

YOU WILL NEED

wooden batten, window
width plus 10cm (4in)
either side

spirit level

drill

wallplugs and screws

screwdriver

milliner's velvet in dark
green and pink

scissors

staple gun

tape measure

2 or more artificial cabbages
on wire stems

one *Screw the batten above the window. Cut two pieces of green velvet to length and staple them to the batten in pleats, so that they meet in the middle.*

two *Cut two rectangular pieces of green velvet, roughly 1½ times the width of the window. Bunch them up and staple them across the top. Scrunch the pink velvet into three large roses and staple to the top of the pelmet.*

three *Staple the stems of the wire cabbages to the walls on either side of the windows. Then roll the curtains into twists and tuck behind the cabbages. Pull the cabbages in front of the curtains and staple in place.*

HANGING AROUND

MAKE THE PRETTIEST of chandelier-hangings with simple deciduous twigs such as apple or pear branches. Select a few branches with gnarled, interesting shapes and bind them together to make a pleasing structure, then hang the finished chandelier in the centre of a window, suspended from a length of gold cord. Trim the branches with eye-catching trinkets such as crystal droplets and tiny pearls, all fixed with the finest of gold twine. This project would also look stunning hanging from a ceiling rose or as a wall decoration.

YOU WILL NEED

2–3 apple or pear tree branches

fine gold wire

scissors

gold cord

crystal droplets

gold beading wire

small pearls

gilded decorations

one *Take the branches and move them around until they form a pretty shape. Bind the branches together at the top with fine gold wire.*

two *Attach a length of gold cord to hang the branches.*

three *Thread crystal droplets on to gold wire. Make short strings of pearls.*

four *Wire the remaining decorations, then twist the wires to make hanging loops. Position the twig chandelier and hang on the jewels.*

Walls and Floors

Parchment Paper Art ♦ Coloured String ♦ Panels and Stamp Motif

Punched Tin Wall ♦ Fabric Wall ♦ Brown Paper Panelling

Cork-Stamped Floor ♦ Fake Animal-Skin Rug ♦ Faux-Soapstone Floor

Rubber Mats ♦ Checked Floor Mats ♦ Photocopy Montage

Stencilled Hardboard ♦ Pop-Art Floor ♦ Studded Floor

$\mathcal{I}$NTRODUCTION

HOW OFTEN HAVE YOU LOOKED at your rather tired walls and thought about giving them a lift? How often have you looked at a jaded old carpet and wished you could afford an alternative? If lack of time and money have stopped you before, we have the answers for you. Packed with really original and innovative ideas - and without a rag roller or stippler brush in sight - these stylish projects for wall and floor decoration will provide creative inspiration at little cost and in next to no time. Our fabulous treatments go far beyond simple paint effects and are totally original: from using photocopies for a graphic black and white effect, draping fabric to disguise an irregular surface, creating mosaics from broken china, or applying solid panels of colour to liven up a neutral space. Applying simple paper cut-outs, designing your own stencils,

Below left: Geometric patterns in coloured string provide a pleasingly modern and tactile solution to a plain wall. Continue the theme in your furnishings and set off the wall with a traditional wood-and-string chair.

Below right: Studs positioned at regular intervals break up a wooden floor and add interesting detail.

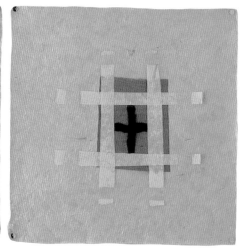

hanging fabric - all these projects will provide a rich source of ideas to help you make the most of colours and textures, and are all illustrated with the help of simple, step-by-step photographs. Floors are expensive to replace, so decisions have to be made carefully. All you need to follow our eye-catching projects is a clean, flat, level surface. If you are working on bare boards, check that they are securely fixed to their joists. Sand boards down with coarse sandpaper - or hire a sanding machine - before commencing work. We have up-to-the-minute ideas for every type of floor in your house - laying carpet tiles to resemble a board game, or creating a marbled-effect or stencilled floor.

Above: Simple cut-outs made from coloured and textured paper add instantly interesting detail to any wall.

Left: You don't need to spend your life savings on building up an art collection–this photocopy montage looks very impressive and won't put a dent in your pocket.

Parchment Paper Art

THERE IS SUCH AN INTERESTING VARIETY of textured and coloured papers available from ordinary stationery stores as well as specialist art and craft suppliers that it is easy to find the right basic ingredients to make some simple but extremely effective pictures, without being skilled at painting. Choose your colour combination and then make slits in the background paper, through which to weave the contrasting colours. These contrasting papers don't need to be clean-cut; in fact, tearing their edges actually enhances the finished look.

YOU WILL NEED
parchment paper sheets
coloured paper sheets
scrap paper
pencil
metal ruler
craft knife
self-healing cutting mat

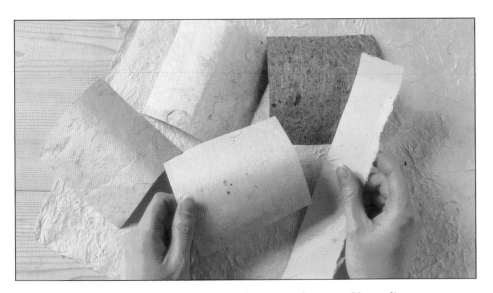

one *Decide on the most interesting combination of papers. Use ordinary scrap paper to plan your design first before cutting the parchment.*

two *Draw lines on the scrap paper where you want the slits to be.*

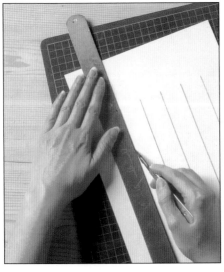

three *Laying the paper on the cutting mat, cut these slits carefully with the craft knife.*

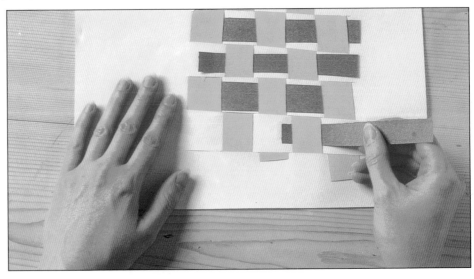

four *Weave paper through the slits. When you are happy with the design, rework using parchment.*

Coloured string

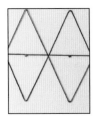

THE IDEA OF DECORATING a wall with coloured string wound around tacks might evoke thoughts of nursery-school crafts; but it's surprising what wonderfully graphic patterns and eye-catching designs you can achieve with this simple technique. Set out a grid of tacks on the wall – substitute picture tacks if the wall won't take ordinary ones – and then you are set to create any design you want. Just wind the string around tightly and evenly, either running the decoration across a wall from side to side or using it to make interesting borders.

YOU WILL NEED

spirit level

straight edge

pencil

tacks

tack hammer

emulsion paint to match existing wall colour

paintbrush

coloured string

one *Lightly draw a grid on the wall, using the spirit level, straight edge and pencil.*

two *Knock in the tacks to the same depth at all the cross points of the grid and all around the outside edges.*

three *Paint out the pencil lines with emulsion paint in the existing wall colour.*

four *Arrange the string. Either buy coloured string or dip plain string in coloured paint to get exactly the colours you want. Wind the string tightly around the tacks, and start and finish with neat loops.*

PANELS AND STAMP MOTIF

BRING LARGE AREAS OF DECORATION to a wall with these easy panels. Painting or dragging panels over a base coat quickly gives interest to large expanses of wall. It's a good idea to connect the panel and wall area outside visually with a simple motif. This could be a strong modern shape, wavy lines or even flowers. The colour of the walls and the style of the motif give scope for a wide range of different looks from the same basic treatment and, of course, you can vary the size of the panel to fit the shape and dimensions of the room.

YOU WILL NEED

emulsion paint in cream, white and black

paint roller

paint-mixing tray

spirit level

straight edge

pencil

masking tape

dragging brush

scrap paper

scissors

high-density foam

glue

craft knife

tape measure

old plate

small roller

one *Give the wall a base coat of cream emulsion paint. Using the spirit level and straight edge, draw the panels on the wall when it is dry.*

two *Mask off the outer edge of the panels with masking tape. Drag white emulsion paint over the base coat.*

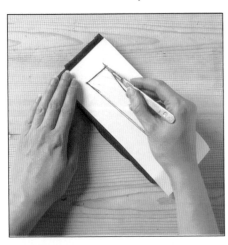

three *Design the motif on paper. Stick the motif to the foam. With the craft knife, cut out the unwanted areas of the design to leave a raised stamp.*

four *Decide on the spacing of the stamps and lightly mark the positions on the wall.*

five *Put some black paint on to the plate and evenly coat the small roller. Roll the paint on to the stamp. Stamp the design in the marked positions.*

PUNCHED TIN WALL

PUNCHED TIN DESIGNS are surprisingly interesting and effective. They are a standard technique of folk-art interiors, but in this context they are often kept to quite small areas. However, there's no reason why punched tin can't be used over a much larger area, where it will look much more dramatic and exciting. You will need to frame the tin in some way, so it makes sense to put it above a dado rail; it could be bordered at the top by a picture rail. Another idea would be to enclose it within mouldings to form a series of matching panels on the wall.

YOU WILL NEED

scrap paper

pencil

thin tin sheet

metal file

long metal ruler

chinagraph pencil

metal punch

tack hammer

wood offcut

drill, with metal and masonry bits

spirit level

straight edge

wallplugs

dome-headed screws

screwdriver

clear varnish or lacquer

varnish brush

one *Design and draw the pattern to scale on paper first. Use a metal file to smooth any rough edges on the metal sheet. Draw the pattern to size on the reverse side of the metal sheet using a chinagraph pencil.*

two *Practise on a spare scrap of metal to get a feel for how hard you need to punch. Punch out the pattern. Put a piece of wood behind the tin to protect your work surface. Drill holes in the corners of the metal sheet.*

three *Using a spirit level and straight edge, draw accurate horizontal guidelines on the wall to indicate the position of the metal sheet. Drill holes in the wall where the corners will be. Insert wallplugs in the holes. Screw the metal sheet securely in position on the wall.*

four *Finish with a protective coat of varnish or lacquer.*

FABRIC WALL

NO SPECIAL SEWING SKILLS are needed to achieve this dramatic wall treatment. Draping fabric on a wall is a good way to disguise lumps and bumps and add a lot of interest for little effort. When you have a modern fabric design, however, such as this eye-catching blanket, it may not seem appropriate to drape it on the wall in baroque folds. Instead, create a contemporary look by pulling it as taut as possible with coloured string at the corners and middle of the fabric.

YOU WILL NEED
tape measure
fabric or blanket
pencil
drill, with masonry bit
wallplugs
screw eyelets
coloured string
matching strong cotton thread

one *Measure the fabric or blanket and mark the positions for the screw eyelets on the wall, bearing in mind that you want the fabric to be pulled very taut. Drill and insert wallplugs at the pencil marks. Screw the eyelets securely into the wall.*

two *Wrap lengths of string tightly around the corners of the fabric and around a small pinch of fabric in the middle of the two long edges.*

three *Feed the strings through the eyelets, pull them tight and secure them by looping the string back on itself and binding it with cotton, for a neat finish.*

BROWN PAPER PANELLING

BROWN PAPER has its own characteristic colour and texture, which look quite wonderful on walls. You can buy it on large rolls, which make papering under a dado rail simplicity itself. Here, the brown paper has been combined with gum arabic adhesive tape for an unusual and elegant interpretation of a classic interior look. You could also add a simple skirting board, using 5 x 2.5cm (2 x 1in) timber.

YOU WILL NEED

brown paper
wallpaper paste
pasting brush
plumb line
pencil
straight edge
paintbrush
gum arabic adhesive
paper roll
spirit level
black beading
glue gun and glue sticks

one *Stick the brown paper, matt side inwards, to the wall. Use wallpaper paste, as if it were wallpaper.*

two *Use a plumb line and straight edge to mark vertical guidelines for the stripes on the brown paper. With a paintbrush, wet the wall in a stripe the width of the gum arabic tape and stick the tape down. Make sure you cover up all the guidelines.*

three *Use a spirit level and straight edge to draw a horizontal guideline for the under-dado border. Stick the tape in place in the same way.*

four *Attach the beading along the top of the border, using the glue gun.*

CORK-STAMPED FLOOR

THIS PRETTY STAMP has been made from seven wine bottle corks. They have been taped together in a daisy shaped bundle and the pattern shapes are cut from the surface of the cork bundle with a scalpel. Dense cork like this is a good material to carve into, being both soft and very smooth. Use the stamp on dust-free sanded wood, or on cork tiles with a dark woodstain. Allow it to stand and soak up the stain for ten minutes then blot it on kitchen paper before you begin printing. Use the paper strips to ensure that the pattern is an even distance from the wall.

YOU WILL NEED

7 wine bottle corks
wood glue or PVA glue
strong adhesive tape
felt-tipped pen
scalpel
2 paper strips of equal width
dark woodstain
bowl
kitchen paper

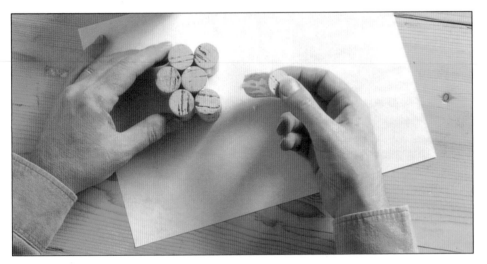

one *Glue the corks in a daisy formation, standing the ends flat on a piece of paper. This will provide a level printing surface. Bind the corks together with strong adhesive tape once the glue has become tacky.*

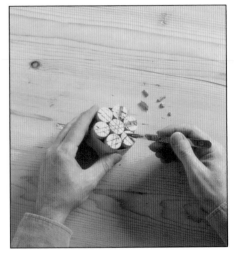

two *Draw the pattern onto the cork surface with a felt-tipped pen. Cut out the background pieces with a scalpel.*

three *Start by making one stamp at each corner, placing the paper spacing strips against the skirting as guides.*

four *Move the strips along the straight skirting board section and stamp a motif about halfway between the first two. Stamp a row of evenly spaced motifs between the existing prints. Continue to stamp a border all round the room.*

Fake Animal-Skin Rug

GIVING A NEW MEANING to the cliché of a baby on a sheep-skin rug, this fun idea could be scaled up for a full-size rug. Rather than making a classical bear-, tiger- or lion-skin rug, be more tongue-in-cheek, with shapes such as prehistoric animals or farm animals. Fake furs now come in a range of wonderfully bright colours, so you could take the concept even further from reality; mix up shapes and patterns.

YOU WILL NEED

large tissue paper sheet
pencil
scissors
long ruler
dressmaker's pins
fake fur fabric
thick felt
pinking shears
iron-on hemming strip
and iron, or sewing machine
or sewing needle and
matching thread

one *Draw a line down the middle of the paper, then draw half the bear shape on one side. Fold in half along the line and cut out the shape.*

two *Enlarge the paper pattern to size then pin it to your fur fabric.*

three *Cut your shape out and then cut the shape out again from the felt, using pinking shears. Include a 6cm (2½ in) allowance all round.*

four *Stick the wrong side of the fur shape to the right side of the felt shape with the hemming strip, or machine or slip stitch the two fabrics together.*

ℱAUX-SOAPSTONE FLOOR

BLACK CORK TILES covering the whole floor in this room were too severe, but when the middle section of the room was treated to this wonderful soapstone effect, they became an important part of the overall grand gesture. The cork tiles in the centre were replaced with a large piece of MDF, to which a maze pattern was applied. This could simply have been painted on to plywood or MDF as a two-dimensional effect, but here the surface has been enhanced by routing the maze pattern (take it to a local joiner; routing really isn't for the inexperienced) and then painted to create a soapstone effect. You could also imitate slate, by using a wave formation and the black leading that was used in the nineteenth century for cleaning cast-iron fireplaces and grates (available from specialist suppliers). Sand or prepare your floor before beginning.

YOU WILL NEED

paper

pencil

MDF sheet

plastic wood or wood filler, if necessary

fine-grade sandpaper

matt emulsion paint: white, dark grey and mid-grey

paintbrushes

wax candle

scraper

softening brush

matt varnish

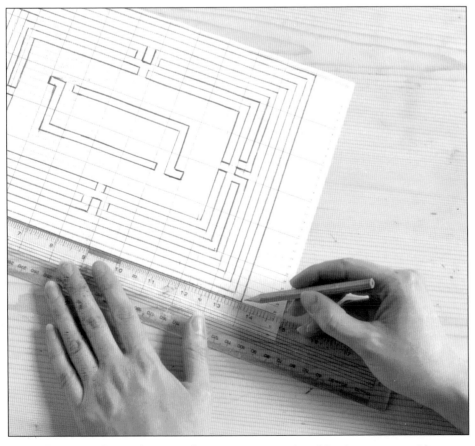

one *On a new floor, plan your design on paper, using this picture as a guide. Draw it on to the sheet of MDF. Take it to a joiner to be routed and ask him to fix it in place on your floor. On an existing floor, draw the maze on the floor directly and ask a joiner to do the routing in situ.*

two *Fill any damage with plastic wood or wood filler, following the manufacturer's instructions. Don't try to achieve a perfectly flush surface at this stage. Leave to dry.*

three *When dry, gently sand until you have a level surface.*

four *Paint the whole surface white and allow it to dry.*

five *Paint over the whole surface of the floor in dark grey.*

six *Using a candle, apply a generous coating of wax with circular movements to the surface of the floor.*

seven *Take off most of the candle wax, using a scraper.*

eight *Follow this with a coat of mid-grey emulsion paint.*

CONTINUED OVER ➤

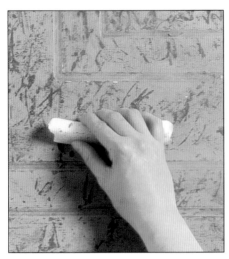

nine *Apply another coat of wax. Take off the wax with the scraper.*

ten *Apply white paint with a dry softening brush, to soften the whole effect. Seal with matt varnish. If you are surrounding the MDF with cork tiles, lay them at the end and butt them up to the edges neatly.*

RUBBER MATS

ABAILABLE FROM RUBBER MANUFACTURERS, this safety matting is valued for its non-slip and protective qualities, and since it is waterproof, it is particularly useful in, say, a shower room. Rubber matting doesn't fray when cut and will happily absorb any lumps or strange joins in a floor. Clean and seal the matting with a silicone spray polish, then fix it in place using any rubber contact adhesive. Make sure your floor is sanded, or lay an MDF layer underneath before starting.

YOU WILL NEED

2 types of rubber safety mat
tape measure
metal rule or straight edge
craft knife
Pirelli rubber tiles in
different patterns
rubber contact adhesive
WD-40 or silicone spray

one *Measure the floor and the rubber matting and carefully trim the matting to size.*

two *For the corners, cut four squares. Divide these diagonally and make four squares by placing two triangles together, with the grooves running across and top to bottom. Position these and the runners around the edge of the room.*

three *Cut pieces from the other matting to fit the central section. Cut the tiles into squares, then cut holes in the mat at regular intervals to take the squares.*

four *Secure all the pieces with rubber adhesive, applied to both surfaces. Spray with WD-40 or silicone spray.*

CHECKED FLOOR MATS

FLOOR MATS ARE EASILY available, extremely cheap and particularly useful as you can usually cut them without their edges fraying. They are manufactured in many finishes, some even incorporating words, symbols or pictures, and all are produced in manageable rectangles. When these heavily textured grey polypropylene mats are arranged with the pile alternately running in different directions, a delightful chequerboard effect is achieved. For a different style of room, you could create a less subtle or even thoroughly funky effect by combining two or more colours. Make sure your floor surface is smooth before starting.

YOU WILL NEED

string

white crayon or chalk

tape measure

grey polypropylene floor mats

long metal ruler or straight edge

craft knife

notched spreader

floor adhesive

one *Use strings stretched across to find the room's centre and mark with a cross. If possible, link the opposite pairs of walls. Measure the floor and work out how many floor mats you will need. Mark the cuts with a white crayon or chalk on the reverse of the floor mats.*

two *If the mats are of carpet quality, first score along the lines before cutting them with the craft knife. Then cut the mats to size.*

three *Using a notched spreader, apply floor adhesive to the floor.*

four *Starting at the centre, carefully lay the mats in position, remembering that, for the chequerboard effect shown here, you need to alternate the weaves.*

PHOTOCOPY MONTAGE

THIS EFFECT IS REMINISCENT of the wonderful painted floors of the great European palaces. Few of us can afford to commission frescoes and floor painting, but we might still aspire to a home decorated in a style fit for Marie Antoinette. Using photocopied images on a freshly prepared floor can turn these dreams into reality. Choose any theme: the photograph shows a composition of landscapes, but architectural drawings, classical motifs, such as columns, garden urns and statues, or even still-lives of fruit or vegetables could be made into successful montages. Using the same techniques, you could create a totally modern feeling using colour photocopies of, say, flower heads; instead of stencilling the borders, add freehand leaves and scrolls if you are skilled.

YOU WILL NEED

cream and green eggshell
emulsion paint

paintbrushes

photocopied images

long metal ruler

craft knife

self-healing cutting mat

artist's watercolour or
acrylic paints

gum arabic tape
(optional)

pencil

masking tape

acetate sheet

bleed-proof paper
(such as tracing paper)

green stencil paint

stencil brush

wallpaper paste

matt varnish

one *Starting with a well-prepared hardboard or marine-plywood floor, paint on an undercoat of cream eggshell paint, followed by a top coat. Allow to dry completely.*

two *Experiment with images in different sizes and settle on an arrangement that looks good on your floor. Trim the images so that you are left with just the pictures.*

three *If your images are black and white, use watercolour or acrylic paints to put soft washes of colour over the prints. You may need to stretch the paper, using gum arabic tape, depending on the quality of the paper (test a small area first).*

four *Arrange the images on the floor and plan and draw out the borders. Mask off the boxes for the images with masking tape. Paint between the lines of masking tape with green eggshell paint. When the paint is almost dry, gently peel off the masking tape.*

five *Make the stencil from the acetate sheet. Apply the stencil to the floor with masking tape and stipple with green paint. Glue the photocopies to the floor with wallpaper paste. Varnish the floor several times.*

STENCILLED HARDBOARD

DAMAGED OR IRREGULAR FLOORS are frequently covered in hardboard and you may feel that this smooth, hard surface is especially in keeping if you have adopted a modernist, minimalist approach to decorating. If you discover hardboard in mint condition, in most instances it is not wise to lift it, as it is probably hiding some horror below. However, with several coats of varnish, hardboard has a natural patina of its own, which is very appealing and works as a neutral background as well as a wooden floor does. Introduce additional interest by using stencils, which here mimic a rather fifties-style rug, although the brown hardboard would suit different colours. The contrast of black or white works well; choose a bold, non-figurative pattern.

YOU WILL NEED

metal ruler or straight edge

pencil

paper

black water-based paint

paintbrushes

masking tape

self-healing cutting mat

acetate sheet

craft knife

pin

stencil brush

lint-free cloth or fine-grade sandpaper (optional)

eraser

gloss varnish

one *Draw the border motif to the desired size on paper.*

two *Photocopy the design and make sure that the repeat works, by placing several sheets together.*

three *Work out a right-angled section for the corners. Make sure it ties in neatly with the repeat on both sides.*

four *Black in the design and photocopy it. Lay the copies around the floor, to ensure that your design will fit pleasingly, and experiment until you have an effect you are happy with.*

five *With pencil, mark the outer edge of your border on the floor (in the photograph, this is about 13cm (5½in) from the edge of the room).*

six *Draw out pencil guidelines for your border all round the room.*

seven *Stick one of the photocopies, with masking tape, to the cutting mat. Tape the acetate sheet over it.*

eight *Using the steel ruler and holding the knife at an angle, carefully cut out the stencil. To help get neat, sharp corners, make a pin prick just at the corner first; this also helps to prevent you from cutting too far.*

nine *With masking tape, attach the stencil to the hardboard, lining it up carefully with your guidelines.*

ten *Using a stencil brush, stipple in the neat black triangles, making sure that the paint is very dry so that it does not seep under the stencil.*

CONTINUED OVER ➤

eleven *Lift up the stencil and re-position it for the next section. Remember to make sure the underside of the stencil is clear of paint. If you need to mask certain areas of the stencil so that you continue the repeat when working the corners, do this with a piece of paper held firmly in place with masking tape.*

twelve *If you make a mistake or smudge the stencilling, rub it clean with a damp cloth or, if the surface is more porous, very gently sand away the paint when dry. Finally, remove the guidelines with an eraser and seal the floor with at least two coats of varnish.*

POP-ART FLOOR

MUCH INSPIRATION for interior decoration is to be gleaned from the pop artists of this century, with their whimsical approach to art. These naïve shapes painted on a large surface make use of the pop-art conventions of sheer boldness and simplicity, with multiple repetitions of strong images rather than intricate busyness. Dramatically discordant colours – orange and shocking pink in this case – are the most appropriate. This idea works best on a concrete floor.

YOU WILL NEED

white matt emulsion paint

paint roller

tape measure

pencil

masking tape

blue, red, shocking pink and
orange matt emulsion paint

PVA glue or acrylic varnish

one *Give the floor two coats of white emulsion, to ensure that the colours of the design ring bright and true.*

two *Measure and draw out your design. Mask off the border, which needs to be crisply painted. Do the same along the outside of the star.*

three *Paint the star, then fill in the area inside the border; masking may not be necessary as a little white space between the star and border and background makes it look as though silk-screening has been used – a technique common in pop art. Seal the floor with diluted PVA glue or acrylic varnish.*

STUDDED FLOOR

CREATE THE APPEARANCE of the deck of a battleship in your bathroom, with studs positioned at regular intervals across the floor and painted in battleship grey. Alternatively, you could leave the wood natural and studs unpainted. The broad silver studs used here are called "domes of silence", because they are designed to fit under chair legs to help them glide smoothly across the floor without making a noise. However, you can choose any studs, as long as they are sturdy enough to withstand the traffic on the floor and they are not sharp or liable to damage shoes or furniture. Sand the floor carefully before commencing.

YOU WILL NEED
pencil
steel ruler or straight edge
studs or "domes of silence"
eraser
acrylic varnish (optional)
paintbrush (optional)
tack hammer
cloth, softwood block or carpet scrap
wood glue (optional)

one *Decide on the spacing and pattern of the studs or domes. Draw diagonal grid lines in accordance with your design and mark with a little cross where each stud is to go.*

two *Rub out all markings, except the crosses. If necessary, apply a couple of coats of acrylic varnish to the whole floor, to seal the wood.*

three *Using a hammer and something soft, such as a folded cloth or softwood block, to prevent damage to the studs, hammer them in over the crosses. If you use "domes of silence", which have relatively shallow teeth, hammer them in only half way to start with. Remove the domes, apply a little wood glue and then replace them and hammer them in all the way. This technique can be used on any decorative wooden floor.*

Beds and Bedding

Lovely Linens ◆ Trimmed Cushions ◆ Victorian Lace ◆ Canopied Bed

Beach Mat Bed ◆ Romantic Netting ◆ Black and White Prints

Animal Cushions ◆ Dream Trellis ◆ Love Pillows ◆ Gingham Headboard

Chintz Headboard ◆ Entwined Headboard ◆ Hammock Quilt

Tartan Bedhead ◆ Renaissance Headboard

INTRODUCTION

YOU CAN ACHIEVE INSTANT soft-furnishing style with minimum effort with the help of these sumptuous ideas. In the bedroom, let your personal style have a free rein and really go to town with our instant and dramatic bed-dressing effects. We also show you how to fill the whole house with stylish and original cushions. If you don't know a four-poster from a half-tester, or have always fancied a futon but didn't know quite what to put on it, then we have the answers for you. This is spontaneous and creative interior design for people with more imagination than skill who want the opportunity to try something a little unusual. There are lots of ideas for dressing up basic beds and none of the projects require advanced DIY or soft-furnishing skills - but they do promise dramatic transformations. Tools and special equipment have been kept to a minimum - the only two indispensable items are a staple gun and a glue gun. These two tools provide freedom from conventional methods of construction, fixing and draping, and allow you to achieve

Above: Fake animal prints are both post-modern and witty. If your public face is respectable and restrained, let yourself go in the privacy of the boudoir and mix and match spots and stripes as much as you please.

Left: Remember, we spend one third of our lives in bed, so the surroundings should be as delightful as possible. Customize your cushions and scatter them on beds, in armchairs and even on the floor to create a space that is ideal for reading, contemplating or just lounging.

the impossible - and keep it there. Bed dressing can mean just what the name suggests - giving a jaded divan a new set of covers - or it can mean making a bedhead, hanging up drapes or even building a four-poster frame, which isn't as daunting as it sounds! Follow our fabulous ideas with cushions to liven up a neglected sofa or armchair or to throw them over your newly revamped bed. Whichever project you choose, simply follow the clear and easy step-by-step instructions and transform your chosen object for a very limited outlay.

Right: You don't have to be Scottish to appreciate this treatment. A tartan bed-head takes very little effort to make and is a perfect alternative to feminine frills. Hang your tartan from a rail to disguise a plain or uneven wall, protect the sleeper from night-time draughts and provide a focal point for the room all in one.

LOVELY LINENS

PRETTY UP PERFECTLY PLAIN LINENS with splashes of vibrant colour. To add definition, run strips of rick-rack edging around; for frilliness, buy broderie anglaise and sew this on to the pillowcase. You could weave tapestry wool through the broderie in place of ribbon, to add colour. Alternatively, look for linens which have a fine-holed edging and thread through this with fine tapestry wool. To complement the edges, add tiny decorative crosses to buttons sewn on to the pillowcase. A more time-consuming, but extremely effective decoration is made by scalloping the edge of a sheet and decorating with tapestry wool.

YOU WILL NEED

paper

pencil

cardboard

scissors

single or double white sheet

sewing machine

white sewing thread

small, sharp-pointed scissors

red tapestry wool

tapestry needle

plain pillowcase

3m (3 yards) broderie anglaise

dressmaker's pins

needle and tacking thread

buttoned pillowcase, with fine-holed decorative edge

glue gun and glue sticks

decorative red buttons

small cushion, with frilled-edge and centre-opening cover

one *Cut out a cardboard template for the sheet edging. Draw around it then machine satin stitch over the line. Cut along outside the sewn line.*

two *Cut lengths of coloured tapestry wool and knot the ends. Sew the lengths of wool through the sheet leaving the long ends as decoration.*

three *Edge the plain pillowcase with broderie anglaise. Then use a tapestry needle to thread coloured yarn through the holes in the lace. You can also use this technique to decorate pillowcases with fine-holed decorative edging.*

four *You can liven up plain buttons on a pillowcase by using a glue gun to apply decorative coloured buttons on top. Decorate round cloth buttons by making neat cross-stitches over them with tapestry wool.*

TRIMMED CUSHIONS

DRESS UP A PILE OF PLAIN CUSHIONS and transform the atmosphere of your bedroom in an afternoon. The embellishments used here are dressmaker's trimmings which are available in a wide range of materials, shapes, colours and sizes. Upholstery and soft-furnishing trimmings tend to be more expensive and the range is limited, so it is well worth looking out for a dressmaking specialist. Market stallholders often carry haberdashery offcuts, with short lengths of fringing, beading, braids and lace which are ideal for embellishing cushions. Tie tassels and cord around the ends of a bolster cushion, for example, or embellish a plain black cushion with an unusual motif.

YOU WILL NEED

3 cushions: 2 velvet
and 1 silk
fringing
needle and matching threads
pencil
pair of compasses
thin card
scissors
pins
black lace and fringing
black bobble trimmings
tape measure

one *For the first cushion, slip-stitch the ends of a length of fringing, so that it doesn't unravel.*

two *Cut a quarter circle from thin card and place it on the cushion as a guide for the curve of the fringing. Slip-stitch along the edge of the fringing using a matching thread.*

three *For the second cushion, pin three or four parallel rows of black lace and fringing on to a yellow-ochre velvet cushion.*

four *Slip-stitch the trimmings in place with matching thread.*

five *For the third cushion stitch two rows of black bobble trim on to an orange silk cushion. Pin one row then use a tape measure to align the second.*

Victorian Lace

NOTHING LOOKS MORE ROMANTIC and feminine than a brass bed covered with snowy white, lace-trimmed bed linen. Make layers of scallops and frills on sheets, bolsters, pillows and bedcovers. Start by buying a good cotton duvet cover with a scalloped edge. Trawl second-hand shops and flea markets for lace-edged tablecloths, dressing table runners, tray cloths and curtain panels. Look out for old white cotton sheets with embroidered edges to add interest.

YOU WILL NEED

plain white bed linen

selection of lacy tablecloths, tray cloths, mats, chair backs or dressing table runners

pins

iron

iron-on hemming tape or needle and white thread

bolsters

rubber bands

white ribbon or raffia

one *Select suitably sized lace additions to make central panels or corner details on the pillow-cases and duvet cover. Pin them in position.*

two *Use iron-on hemming tape and an iron to bond the two layers together, or slip-stitch them in place.*

three *Roll the bolster up in a lace-edged tablecloth and bunch up the ends, securing them with rubber bands. Tie ribbon or raffia over the gathered ends and drape the lace edging.*

CANOPIED BED

A SIMPLE DRAPED CANOPY is a great way to define and decorate a sleeping area without completely enclosing it. The muslin is draped over a wooden plant support. The natural rustic character of the twigs combines very well with the unfussy appearance of unbleached muslin. Muslin is inexpensive, so buy more than you need – any extra will make a pretty cascade at the end of the bed.

YOU WILL NEED

at least 12m (12 yd)
unbleached muslin

iron-on hemming tape

iron

rustic plant support

rubber bands

twine

scissors

ceiling hook

one *Turn up a hem at each end of the fabric and use iron-on hemming tape to make a neat hem. Find the middle of the fabric length and bunch and wrap the muslin around the narrow end of the plant support at this point.*

two *Pull the fabric into a pleasing shape, then secure it with rubber bands. Wind the twine to cover the rubber bands and decorate the fabric.*

three *Attach a ceiling hook centrally above the bed. Hang the plant support from it. Drape the muslin either side of the support and over the bed ends.*

BEACH MAT BED

A SIMPLE FOUR-POSTER FRAME can be built to fit around an existing base and mattress. This requires only basic carpentry skills as the timber can be cut to size when you buy it, and just needs drilling and screwing together. The wood used here is basic construction timber that has been left in its natural state, but you could colour it with woodstain or paint it to co-ordinate with the decor of the bedroom.

Grass beach mats are perfect for hanging around the four-poster, especially if your room is decorated with natural fabrics and earth colours. The loosely stitched grass strips allow a soothing, soft golden light to filter through and the air to circulate.

YOU WILL NEED

grass beach mats

packet of brass paper fasteners

rough twine

scissors

odd-shaped shells, pebbles and driftwood

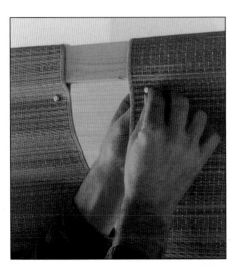

one *Fold one short edge of each beach mat over the top rail of the four-poster frame. Push paper fasteners through the mats just below the rail and open out the prongs. Use four fasteners along the top of each beach mat.*

two *The mats are edged with different coloured tape that makes fine stripes around the bed. Arrange the mats to make the most of this striping.*

three *Decide how many blinds you want to tie up – maybe all, or just a select few. You will need about 1m (1 yd) of rough twine for each mat to be rolled up. Cut the lengths required and tie some shells, pebbles and bits of driftwood randomly along the length and at each end of the twine.*

four *Dangle over the top rail and use them to tie back the rolled-up blinds.*

ROMANTIC NETTING

EVEN IF YOU HAVE NO practical need for mosquito netting, the light and airy beauty of this project makes it ideal for the bedrooms of urban romantics who dream of being in the Punjab or on the Serengeti plains. Netting like this can be bought from camping shops and comes complete with a spoked wooden coronet that opens like a fan to support it. Here, the spokes have then been decorated with dangling glass ornaments to make the netting look more exotic than utilitarian. Plain white netting is very appealing, but it can also be dyed in any pale colour.

YOU WILL NEED

mosquito netting, with coronet and fixings

dangling glass ornaments and earrings

fine wire

long-nosed pliers

ceiling hook

one *Fan out the spokes of the wooden coronet and fit them into the channels of the netting.*

two *Thread assorted glass ornaments, beads and earrings on to lengths of fine wire to make decorative pendants.*

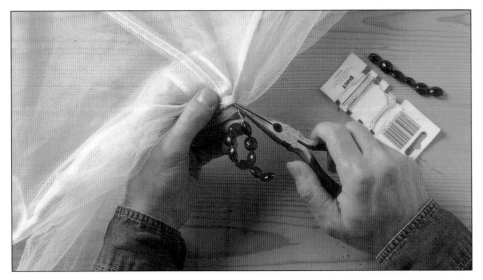

three *Thread the wire ends through the netting at the bottom of the spokes. Use long-nosed pliers to twist the ends together to secure them.*

four *Attach the ring and rope provided to the centre of the coronet. Hang the net from a ceiling hook above the bed.*

BLACK AND WHITE PRINTS

IMAGINE BEING ABLE to decorate soft furnishings with any image or picture of your choice. There is now a special transparent gel available which enables you to transfer black and white or colour images on to fabric. The image can then be sealed to make it resistant to wear and tear. By enlarging or reducing the images on a photocopier, you can obtain a selection of prints that will fit perfectly on to any item that you would like to decorate, such as cushions, pillows or even a quilt. You can use the same process to monogram your bed linen in royal style. However, because the image will be reversed once it is transferred, you will have to photocopy any lettering on to acetate first.

YOU WILL NEED

photocopies of chosen images

scissors

plain-coloured cotton cushion cover

iron

plastic carrier bag

image-transfer gel

paintbrush

soft cloth

sheet of acetate (optional)

one *Choose your images and make the required number of copies. Here, several copies of the same image are used to form a frame around the portrait.*

two *Cut away all the excess paper, leaving only the images that you want to transfer.*

three *To design the cushion cover, arrange the images on a flat surface. Experiment with spacing until you are happy with the design.*

four *Pre-wash and iron the cushion cover. This is important because glazes used to stiffen fabrics may adversely affect the transfer process. Place the cover on a plastic carrier bag to protect your work surface.*

five *Paint a thick layer of transfer gel on to the first photocopy, making sure that you have covered it completely.*

six *Place the image face-down in position on the cushion cover and gently rub all over the back with a soft cloth. Leave the image in position.*

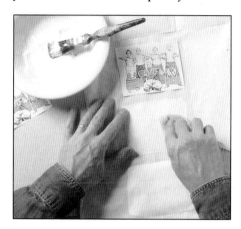

seven *Repeat steps 5 and 6 with all the images, ensuring that they are positioned accurately before you make contact with the fabric. Leave to transfer overnight.*

eight *Soak the cloth with clean water and then use the wet cloth to saturate the photocopy paper.*

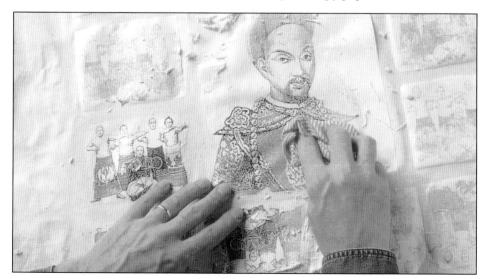

nine *Keep the cloth wet and begin to rub away the paper, working from the centre outwards. The images will have transferred on to the fabric. When all the paper has been removed, leave the fabric to dry.*

ten *Apply a final fixing coat of the transfer gel to the prints and leave to dry completely.*

CONTINUED OVER ➤

eleven *You can use the same process to monogram your bed linen. Photocopy the initials on to a sheet of acetate. Then turn the acetate over and photocopy from the acetate on to paper to reverse. Cut out the print.*

twelve *Transfer the initials as described in steps 5 to 10. The transfer process will reverse the initials once more, so that they are now the right way round.*

ANIMAL CUSHIONS

ANIMAL PRINTS HAVE NEVER BEEN more popular and the quality of fake fur now available is truly fantastic. It is also a delight to animal-lovers and the environmentally conscious. The distinctive boldness of the cowhide print chosen here makes great cushion covers.

This low bed is draped with lengths of silky smooth velvet tiger- and leopard-skin fabric that spill over on to the floor, adding to the tactile, languorous atmosphere. This project doesn't have to be a permanent fixture, so bring out this special bedding for wild weekends – and it may bring out the animal in you!

YOU WILL NEED

card

scissors

button blanks

small pieces of black velvet

hemmed squares of cowhide print, 5cm (2in) smaller than the cushions

black velvet cushions

needle and thread

tiger- and leopard-skin fabrics

one *Cut a circle of card approximately 1cm (½in) larger all round than the button blanks. Use the card pattern to cut circles of black velvet.*

two *Cover the top of each button blank with a velvet circle, tucking in the edges so that they catch on to the spikes underneath.*

three *Press the backing firmly in place to make neatly covered black velvet buttons.*

four *Stitch a hemmed cowhide fabric square diagonally on each cushion. Sew a black button on to the centre, stitching through both the cowhide print and the black velvet cushion. Arrange the tiger- and leopard-skin fabrics over the bed.*

DREAM TRELLIS

DRESS UP A PLAIN WALL behind a simple bed with a most unusual trellis headboard made from woven twigs and branches. The trellis is very lightweight and is easily fixed in place. Continue the theme with twig accessories, ranging from chairs to cache-pots, and complement the decor with crisply starched white sheets and pretty cushion covers.

Country garden centres are always worth a visit, because trellis-work like this is handmade and producers often use local garden centres as outlets. Alternatively, you might like to try your own hand.

YOU WILL NEED

garden raffia

scissors

handmade twig trellis

masonry nails or
cavity wall fixtures

hammer

one *Divide the raffia into two bunches of approximately twelve strands each. Knot one end of each bunch.*

two *Plait the strands to make two braids about 10cm (4in) long.*

three *Tie the plaits on to the trellis 25cm (10in) from each end. Attach the plaits to the wall above the bed, suspending the trellis behind the bed.*

LOVE PILLOWS

MAKE SURE THE RIGHT message gets across by stencilling the word 'love' on your pillows in both English and French, the archetypal language of romance! The typeface used is the graphic designer's favourite, Gill (bold), chosen for its stylish simplicity and clarity. There is no doubt what is meant here. The word has been enlarged on a photocopier to 18cm (7in) long. You can adapt this idea for other messages that are completely personal and private, but if you have children, discretion may be a good idea. Choose colours that match your bedroom's overall scheme or that are your favourites. Fabric paints are available in a wide range of colours. Always wash and iron the fabric before stencilling to rid it of any glazes that could block the colour absorption.

YOU WILL NEED
photocopied enlargement
of the words
spray adhesive
2 pieces of stencil cardboard
scalpel or craft knife
cutting mat or thick cardboard
sheet of thin cardboard
white cotton pillow cases
fabric paint
plate
stencil brush
iron

one *Enlarge the templates to the required size. Spray the backs of the photocopies with spray adhesive and stick them on to the stencil card.*

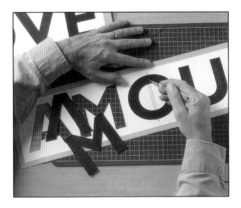

two *Cut out the letters on a cutting mat. The O, A and R need ties to retain the internal letter features, so draw them in "bridges" before you cut out.*

three *Place a sheet of thin cardboard inside the pillow case, so that the colour does not bleed through to the other side.*

four *Apply paint sparingly to letters. You can always build up colour later, but too much paint can cause problems. When dry, seal with a hot iron.*

AEOL
MRUV

GINGHAM HEADBOARD

THIS HEADBOARD CONVERSION creates a fresh new style with added comfort. Gingham always looks crisp and bright, so you will wake up bright-eyed and ready to face the day. It is available in both small and large checked patterns and in a wide variety of both bright and pastel colours. The gingham is backed with quilter's wadding. Alternatively, you could use other fabrics to create a different sort of mood – a small floral print for a feminine, country cottage decor or a vibrant primary colour for a teenager's room, for example. The headboard should be rectangular in shape and can be solid or of a slatted or spindled type. Measure the width and height of the headboard, then double the height measurement so that the gingham folds in half over the top.

YOU WILL NEED

iron-on quilter's wadding

dressmaker's scissors

iron

gingham, width of the headboard x twice the height, plus seam allowance on all edges

iron-on hemming tape

needle and matching sewing thread

2 metres (2 yards) red ribbon

pins

tape measure

one *Cut the wadding to the size of the headboard. Press one end of the gingham on to the wadding. The other end of the gingham will fold over the headboard back. Leave a large seam allowance all around the edge.*

two *Fold the seams over and tuck the corners in neatly. Use iron-on hemming tape or a needle and thread to secure the edges. As the hems will be on the inside of the cover, they will not be visible.*

three *To make the ties, cut the ribbon into 16 equal lengths.*

four *Pin, then sew four ribbons, equally spaced, along the inside edges of each side of the cover. Fold the cover over the headboard and tie the ribbons in bows to finish.*

CHINTZ HEADBOARD

GIVE YOUR PADDED HEADBOARD a new lease of life using old chintz curtains. The fabric improves with age as the colours fade and mellow delightfully, and it looks wonderful teamed with crisp white cotton, handmade quilts or plaid woollen blankets in a traditional bedroom. Use the very best section of pattern for the bedhead and tuck remaining lengths under the mattress to form a valance. If you prefer a more permanent valance, you could sew pleated lengths of the same chintz fabric around the edges of a fitted sheet.

YOU WILL NEED

pair of floral chintz curtains
scissors
tape measure
headboard
pencil
staple gun and staples

one *Trim the curtains to get rid of any thick seams, curtain tape and bulky hems. Cut a strip of curtain long enough to fold over the front and on to the back of the headboard at the sides, top and bottom. Smooth it over the front of the headboard then move to the back. Draw any curved corners on to the back of the fabric.*

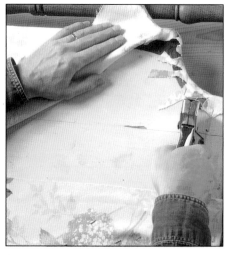

two *Cut notches in the fabric right up to the drawn line, so that the fabric will fit the curve without puckering. Staple each cut strip on to the headboard.*

three *Pull down the top flap tautly and staple it on to the headboard.*

four *Pull up the bottom flap tautly and staple it in place. Staple both side edges in the same way. Cut a panel of fabric to cover all the stapled edges on the back. Turn in the edges and staple the panel flat on to the backing board.*

ENTWINED HEADBOARD

QUITE APART FROM BEING one of the most stylish looks around, rope wrapping is a real pleasure to do. All you need is a frame, which can be a junk-shop find or a DIY structure made from construction timber. The wood is completely hidden by the coils of rope, so there is no need to prepare the surface in any way. Rope comes in many different twists and thicknesses, some more decorative than others. Some ropes are made from natural fibres and others, like the one used here, are synthetic. An advantage of synthetic rope is that the ends can be sealed by holding them over a flame to melt the fibres together.

YOU WILL NEED

rope

wooden-framed headboard

tape measure

pen

scissors or craft knife

cutting mat or thick cardboard

lighter or matches (optional)

glue gun and glue sticks

one *To calculate the length of rope needed to wrap each wooden post, first divide the height of the post by the thickness of the rope. Multiply this figure by the circumference of the post. Mark the rope at this point.*

two *Cut the lengths of rope required to wrap all the posts. If you are using synthetic rope, seal the ends by holding them briefly over a flame. Use the glue gun to stick the end of the rope to the back of the first post to be wrapped.*

three *Wrap the rope tightly around the post, keeping the coils as close together as possible. To maintain the tension, apply a few dabs of hot glue.*

four *Cut short lengths of rope to cover gaps and another to cover loose ends and blobs of glue at the intersection. Glue the ends at the back of post.*

five *Make sure that all the intersections are finished in the same way so that the symmetry is maintained. Finish off with rope decorations.*

Hammock Quilt

RECLINING IN A HAMMOCK MAY BE THE ULTIMATE relaxation, but it is only really possible to lie back and enjoy the sway if you feel completely secure. So make quite sure that your wall fittings are sturdy and properly installed and that the wall itself is strong enough to take the strain. Use strong metal garage hooks with long screws and heavy-duty wallplugs. Once the safety angle has been covered, you can then turn your attention to comfort and make this stylish and simple no-sew quilt to dress up your hammock and keep you cosy.

YOU WILL NEED

iron

2.5 m (2¾ yd) iron-on wadding

5 m (5½ yd) blue fabric

2.5 m (2¾ yd) black cotton fabric

scissors

tape measure

iron-on hemming tape

5 m (5½ yd) black iron-on mending tape

pins

one *Iron the wadding to one half of the wrong side of the blue fabric. Then fold the other half over so that the wadding is sandwiched by the blue fabric. This will give the quilt some thickness. Next, cut the black fabric into four 14cm (5½in) wide strips to fit the quilt edges. Press a 1cm (½in) hem along the long edges. Iron each strip in half to make a long doubled strip 6cm (2¼in) wide. This will be used to border the blue cloth. Place a length of iron-on hemming tape along each edge of the blue fabric and enclose each edge with a doubled black border strip. Iron to bond the fabrics. Fold down the corners of the black edging to achieve a mitred effect. Turn the fabric over and repeat on the other side.*

two *Cut twenty-four 20cm (8in) strips of iron-on mending tape and use the tape measure to position them on the quilt in four rows of three crosses.*

three *Pin the crosses in place if required, then iron them in position.*

TARTAN BEDHEAD

WOOLLEN TARTAN RUGS are real comfort blankets, traditionally used on winter car journeys and picnics. The two rugs used in this project are doubled over, with their folded edges meeting in the middle. To complete the Highland hunting lodge atmosphere, the rugs are hung above the bedhead from a rough-hewn "branch".

YOU WILL NEED

2 matching tartan blankets
or rugs

tape measure

needle

thick contrasting thread

2.5cm (1in) wooden dowel
(slightly longer than the
bed width)

craft knife

fine-grade sandpaper

cloth

shellac

2 iron pipe holders
(to fit 2.5cm (1in) pipe)

drill and wallplugs

screwdriver

kilt pins

one *Fold each blanket in half lengthways and pin together along the folded seam. Blanket stitch the outside edges, then stitch the blankets together along the folded edge. If you don't like sewing, hold the seams closed with three kilt pins.*

two *Start decorating the wooden pole by roughly carving away both ends of the dowel with a craft knife. Sand the rough edges with sandpaper. Use a cloth to rub shellac into the wood.*

three *Screw the pipe holders to the wall. Fix the rail in place. Hang the blankets over the rail, with a 35cm (14in) overlap to make a pelmet, pinning it in place with kilt pins.*

RENAISSANCE HEADBOARD

DRAMATIC EFFECTS HAVE BEEN used in this bedroom to create a very distinctive atmosphere, with the large painting dominating the room. It's a good idea to visit a museum shop for the best range and quality of art posters – you are certain to find something for all tastes. You can apply a crackle glaze or antiquing varnish to the poster if you wish to add an authentically aged Renaissance look.

YOU WILL NEED

wallpaper paste

poster

MDF (width of poster x height of poster plus mattress to floor measurement), plus allowance for frame

paste brush

pencil

ruler

picture rail moulding (height of poster x 2, plus width x 1)

mitring block

small saw

viridian green emulsion paint

paintbrushes

gold spray paint

fine-grade sandpaper

glue gun and glue sticks

crackle-glaze varnish

red artist's oil colour

clean cloths

clear varnish

drill and fixtures to attach MDF to bed frame (depending on the type of bed)

one *Mix up the wallpaper paste. Mark the position of the poster on the MDF and apply paste to that section. Smooth the poster on to the board and leave to dry. Any air bubbles should disappear as the glue dries.*

two *Measure and mark the lengths of moulding for the frame. It goes along the top of the poster and down both sides to mattress height. Saw the corners on a mitring block. Paint a viridian green undercoat. Leave to dry.*

three *Protect your work surface, then spray a coat of gold spray paint over the green. Leave to dry. Rub the frame with fine-grade sandpaper, so that the gold is lifted on the highest ridges to reveal the green beneath. Do not overdo the sanding. Use a glue gun to stick the picture frame around the edges of the poster.*

four *Paint the whole surface of the poster with crackle-glaze varnish, following the manufacturer's instructions. Leave the varnish to crackle. Use a cloth to rub artist's oil colour into the surface. Red is used here but any strong or dark colour will also work well. Rub the oil paint right into the cracks and cover the whole surface.*

five *Rub the oil paint off the surface with a soft cloth. The colour will stay in the cracks. Apply several coats of clear varnish to the poster. When dry, attach the headboard to the bed frame, using the drill and fixtures.*

CHAIRS AND TABLES

Dressing for Dinner ♦ *Pure Plastic*

Tactile Tablecloth

New Ways with Napkins

Egyptian Table-Top

Fabric Swathed Chair ♦ *Astroturf Chair*

Stool with Wood ♦ *Magic Chair*

Rope-Bound Chair ♦ *Space-Age Chairs*

Sheer Fabric Chair ♦ *Fun Fur Chrome Chair*

Polynesian Throne ♦ *Bucket Stool*

Cardboard Chair

INTRODUCTION

Below: Wheat and bamboo trimmings turn a wooden chair into a Polynesian throne reminiscent of the South Seas. Place it in a sunny corner of your garden if you don't have a summer house.

TABLES AND CHAIRS ARE TWO OF THE MOST important elements in every home - they appear in most rooms and in many shapes and forms from the elegant and luxurious to the everyday and useful. Everyone needs somewhere to sit and something to eat off! As they usually grace communal spaces such as kitchens or living rooms, they can suffer more from day to day living - from busy mealtimes, young children or family pets. They are also relatively quick to show wear and tear and very expensive to replace when they start to look a little ragged round the edges. So, if you are short of time and have a limited budget, we will provide simple solutions for instant, affordable and creative table and chair decoration ideas. This thrifty chic is also tremendously satisfying. Easy to follow, step-by-step photographs demonstrate how to paint, glue, tie, pin and staple a wide variety of materials, providing new looks for old favourites. Each project is self-contained and fully illustrated with clear, step-by-step photographs designed for

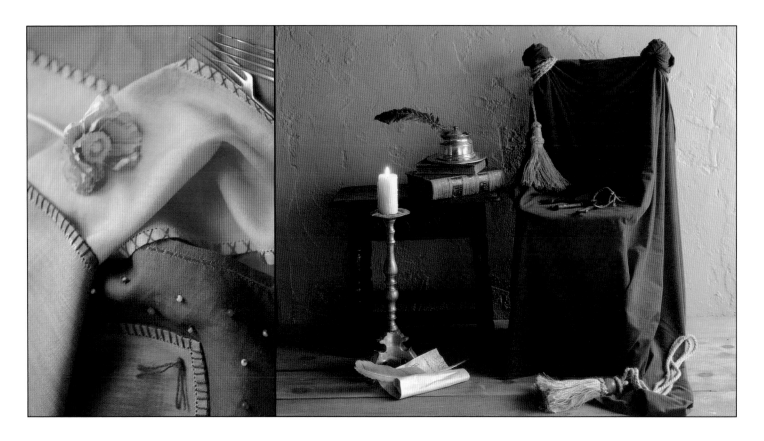

you to use at home. Quite often you will find that furniture needs little more than a new cover or a decorative paint effect to give it a whole new lease of life, so you certainly won't have to think of sacrificing every weekend for months on end to take on a project. And by giving a bit of tender, loving care to an old junk-shop find - bought for next to nothing and revamped equally inexpensively - you can create an individual masterpiece of your own, giving your home a real sense of personal style. So, flick through our wonderful and innovative ideas for paint and fabric treatments and simple embellishments, then arm yourself with a paintbrush or a staple gun … and enjoy!

Above left: Napkins don't have to be white or plain. Embellish bold colours with flower shapes.

Above: Continue this plush fabric and rope treatment with matching tie-backs for toning curtains.

Right: See-through fabric draped over a chair turns the plainest bedroom into a boudoir. White fabric would reflect light back into a dressing-table mirror.

DRESSING FOR DINNER

FOR VERY SPECIAL OCCASIONS, why not dress up your table and chairs. Choose a style of corsage suited to the style of your chairs. A simple unvarnished country chair, for instance, calls for understated trimmings, whereas a fancy French one requires something much more elaborate. Trim the table to match. The individual flower arrangements can be given to your guests to take home. These ideas could not be simpler, but will add to the festivities.

YOU WILL NEED
silk or fresh flowers
fresh greenery
florist's wire
scissors
2.5 m (2.5 yd)
organza ribbon
pot-pourri and star anise
glue gun and glue sticks
fine string
beads

A CHAIR WITH STYLE

one *Use florist's wire to join the flowers together at the stem. Silk flowers are best because they bend as you like.*

two *Continue binding in flowers and greenery, to make an attractive corsage. Trim the stems and tuck in any ends.*

three *Finish with a ribbon bow. Make a wire hook to fix the corsage to the chair.*

LIVENING UP THE TABLE

one *Fill a teapot with pot-pourri. Then cut a circle from organza, fill it with pot-pourri and tie the top with string. Twist a cinnamon stick into the tie and tie the bag to the lid.*

two *Make a necklace for a bottle by pulling apart a piece of fine string into separate strands and glueing star anises to one strand.*

three *Decorate a decanter or jar with a piece of organza ribbon tied into bows, or threaded with beads.*

PURE PLASTIC

A PLASTIC TABLECLOTH is invaluable on a table that gets a lot of use – in a family breakfast room, for example – as it can be wiped clean in seconds and doesn't stain. As a rule, however, ready-made plastic cloths tend to be very plain or extremely garish. To make an attractive as well as practical cloth, why not cut a shaped trim from plain white plastic and make a simple design along the edge using a hole punch? Inexpensive, quick and very easy to make – what could be better? You could also make a matching cloth for a sideboard or serving area.

YOU WILL NEED

tape measure
plastic fabric
dressmaker's scissors
pencil
cardboard
scissors
hole punch
ribbon, string or rope
(optional)

one *Measure your table and cut the plastic fabric to the required size. Draw up and cut out a cardboard template for the scalloped edge. Draw lightly around the template on the wrong side of the plastic fabric with a pencil.*

two *Cut the edging shape with sharp dressmaker's scissors, keeping the scallops rounded and even.*

three *Punch out a design with a hole punch. You could thread ribbon, string or rope through the holes to add even more interest and, perhaps, a splash of colour.*

TACTILE TABLECLOTH

A MASS OF ALL sorts of wonderful trimmings is now available and a trip around the haberdashery department will, with a little imagination, generate any number of ideas. Here, simple upholsterer's webbing was used to edge a plain and practical hessian cloth. The webbing was decorated with string in very loose loops. The charm of this simple design lies in its interesting textures, so it is probably best to use materials in toning colours, as here. However, if you wish, you could make a bold statement in bright primaries or contrasting shades.

YOU WILL NEED
about 2 m (2.5 yd) hessian
dressmaker's scissors
dressmaker's pins
needle and tacking thread
iron
sewing machine and
matching sewing thread
8 m (8¾ yd) webbing
brown string

one *Cut the hessian to the size you require, allowing for hems. Turn under the hems and pin, tack, press and machine-stitch. Cut a length of webbing to go round all four sides. Pin and machine-stitch the webbing around the edge.*

two *Lay the string on the length of webbing and twist it to experiment with different designs – a repeating pattern will look more professional.*

three *Pin, tack and hand-stitch the string to the webbing, to hold it securely. It doesn't matter if there are gaps in the stitching; the looseness of the string is all part of the effect.*

New Ways With Napkins

NAPKINS IN JEWEL-BRIGHT colours add a wonderful and inexpensive splash of brilliance to any dining table and immediately conjure up visions of hotter climates and more exotic places. Choose tapestry wools in strong colours to edge the napkins and trim each one in a different style, adding buttons and beads where appropriate. They will prove really eye-catching used with a plain, boldly coloured tablecloth, country-style china and chunky knives and forks.

YOU WILL NEED
coloured linen napkins
coloured tapestry wools
tapestry needle
large button
about 50 tiny multicoloured beads
tailor's chalk (optional)

one *If your napkin has an open-work edging, work cross-stitch following the decorative holes in the edge. If not, work evenly spaced cross-stitch along the edge. Attach a button with tapestry wool at one corner.*

two *Work the edge of the second napkin in blanket-stitch by holding the thread under the needle and pulling the point of the needle through. Take a few strands of tapestry wool, knot them in the centre and stitch them to one corner.*

three *For the bead edging, work out a design by arranging the beads on a flat surface. You could mark these on the napkin first, by chalking tiny dots where you feel the beads should be. Sew the beads securely in place.*

four *Complete the edging with running stitch. Simply take the thread and weave it in and out of the fabric at regular intervals, to form a pretty line of stitches about 1cm (½in) from the edge.*

EGYPTIAN TABLE-TOP

THE BEAUTY OF THIS TABLE-TOP design lies in its simplicity. Just one colour was used on a bold blue background, with three similar images stamped in regimented rows. The table used here has a lower shelf, but the design would work equally well on an occasional table. The salmon-pink prints show up well on the rich background, making it look even bluer. The stamps are pre-cut and are taken from Egyptian hieroglyphs. The finished table could be the surprising and eye-catching centrepiece of a room decorated in subdued colours.

YOU WILL NEED

3 hieroglyph rubber stamps

ruler and set square

2 card strips, one the length and one the width of the table, for position guides

piece of card or plastic

felt-tipped pen

salmon pink emulsion or acrylic paint

small paint roller

one *Use the stamps and ruler to measure out the stamp positions. Place a card strip along the edge of the table and mark as many stamp lengths as will fit along, leaving even spaces between them. Mark stamp widths along the second card strip.*

two *Position the card strips at 90 degrees to each other to mark the position of the first row. Coat the roller evenly with paint on a piece of card.*

three *Coat the hieroglyphs and stamp in sequence along the first row.*

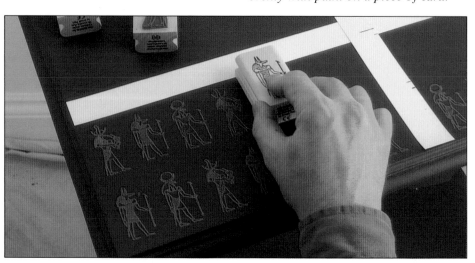

four *Move the wide strip up one stamp space on the short strip, check that it is at 90 degrees and stamp a second row. Continue until the table is covered.*

FABRIC SWATHED CHAIR

THIS EFFECT IS STYLISH and practical and yet needs no sewing skills. None of the usual difficulties caused by the need for washing of fitted covers apply, so you can capitalize on the sheer drama that is created by brilliant white. A generous quantity of fabric is the only essential; this project uses a king-size, pure cotton sheet, which is ready-hemmed, but you can use any wide, preferably washable, fabric that is soft enough to knot and tie. Why not consider this as a stunning addition to your Christmas scheme, by wrapping the dining chairs in red silk?

YOU WILL NEED

chair

fabric

sewing machine
(optional)

one *You need at least twice, and preferably three times, as much fabric as the width of your chair. Hem the fabric, if necessary. Throw the fabric over the chair and centre it.*

two *Tuck fabric down the back behind the seat of the chair. If the chair has arms, do this all around the seat, so that the cover doesn't pull when you sit on the chair.*

three *Sweep the fabric round to the back of the chair, allowing it to drape.*

four *Tie a knot, making sure that the fabric is an even length on both sides and that you have attractive folds and drapes at the sides. Try to tie the knot confidently in one go: otherwise the fabric can look tortured and may be crumpled. Remember that the fabric should cascade down from the knot.*

ASTROTURF CHAIR

CLASSIC CONSERVATORY CHAIRS are usually made of expensive hardwood and are often rather boring and conventional in design. To create a truly modern garden room, therefore, why not jazz up a cheap fifties metal chair with strips of astroturf, available from garden centres and DIY stores. Complete the retro effect with some artificial flowers – although they are as a rule considered kitsch, their use is most definitely tongue-in-cheek here. The chair would also be an ideal talking point for a garden party.

YOU WILL NEED
metal chair
screwdriver
fine- and coarse-grade astroturf
staple gun
ruler
craft knife
glue gun
artificial flowers

one *Unscrew the seat pad and cut a piece of fine-grade astroturf to cover it. Staple it in place.*

two *Measure and cut strips of a coarser grade of astroturf and attach to the seat with a glue gun.*

three *Cut two matching pieces of coarse astroturf to fit over the central back struts of the chair. Glue the artificial flowers to the front piece.*

four *Fix both pieces over the struts with a glue gun.*

STOOL WITH WOOD

THIS IS A VERY SIMPLE and yet effective look, which does not involve any complicated techniques. The wood mouldings used here are available in a considerable range from your local timber merchant or hardware store and are intended for embellishing doors and panelling. However, they also give instant texture to otherwise plain objects, lending them unexpected style.

YOU WILL NEED

wooden stool

white undercoat paint, if necessary

paintbrushes

ruler

pencil

wooden mouldings

glue gun

oil-based brown paint, mixed with 2 parts matt glaze (scumble)

creamy white oil paint

dry brush

one *If your stool is already painted in strong colours, paint it white to give a neutral base colour.*

two *Draw a central grid in pencil on the sides of the stool and decide on the positioning of the mouldings. Stick them on to the surface. Either curves or angles are suitable.*

three *Using the brown glaze and working continuously in one direction (to simulate the grain of the wood), paint the whole stool. Allow to dry.*

four *Using a pale wash of cream, paint over the mouldings. Remove some of the glaze while still wet with a dry brush, to give a limed appearance.*

Magic Chair

COVERED IN NOVA SUEDE, this hard-backed chair has a split personality: a kitsch fifties dining chair by day and a theatrical throne in the evening. Throws are often used to cover easy chairs but the limitless possibilities of using them to add drama to a hard chair, totally changing its appearance, are often overlooked. Another advantage is that you can knot throws and tie them on to the uprights of a hard-backed chair and extras such as tassels or bindings can easily be incorporated.

Any fabric that is wide enough is suitable for this treatment, but squashy fabrics, such as suede or velvet, are particularly stylish. Practicality is not an issue, because the covers can be whisked off to reveal the practical chair underneath.

YOU WILL NEED

hard-backed chair

large piece of plush fabric, for example, Nova suede

tassels and bindings
(optional)

one *Drape the fabric over the chair, making sure it touches the ground at the front.*

two *Take up some excess fabric from the back and form a knot over both chair pegs at the back of the chair.*

three *For further embellishment, secure the corners of the fabric with tassels or bindings.*

ROPE-BOUND CHAIR

COLONIAL-STYLE AND VERANDA CHAIRS have gained considerable popularity recently but, sadly, originals are extremely difficult to find. This is a good technique for a chair whose character would be lost if it were painted or stripped and yet which needs some form of embellishment. Natural trimmings, such as twine, rope or hessian tape, can be expensive, as you will need about 80 metres (90 yards). Look out for less expensive forms of the same product, such as the sash cord used here. You could also use garden twine, rope, washing line or builder's scrim.

YOU WILL NEED

old chair

6 to 8 12m (12yd) bales of sash cord

glue gun

one *Starting at the back of the chair, secure the end of the rope with a small amount of glue from the gun.*

two *Begin wrapping the chair with sash cord, according to your chosen design.*

three *You can use two lengths at a time for the arms, starting with a slip knot.*

four *When you reach the end of the length, secure it by tucking it in at the back of the chair and then glue.*

SPACE-AGE CHAIRS

FOR AN OVERDOSE of the fantastic, create some space-age simplicity and make a statement in your bathroom or kitchen that can't be ignored. Vacuum-formed chairs appeared in vast numbers in our schools and offices, as part of the sixties space-craze. A twenty-first century update can be given to these forgotten and often discarded chairs by adding yet more space-age technology: shiny silver space blankets, used as emergency blankets. These are easily available from most camping shops and their silver appeal is unsurpassed. Vacuum-formed chairs themselves are the classics of their time and crying out for a facelift. Car spray paint is available in many colours if you don't want silver.

YOU WILL NEED

2 plastic chairs
silver car spray paint
PVA glue
paintbrush
1m (1yd) thin wadding
1m (1yd) of 137cm (54in) iridescent lycra fabric
needle and strong thread
scissors
4 ping-pong balls
craft knife
space mat
chinagraph pencil
space blanket

one *Spray the legs of the chairs silver. Apply a coat of PVA glue to the top and underneath of the first chair and stick on the wadding.*

two *Stretch the lycra tautly over the chair. Gather the fabric at the back and stitch it in place. Trim off any excess fabric and turn and tack to neaten the back. Cut holes in the ping-pong balls and insert a leg into each one.*

three *To line the circular hole in the second chair, use the chinagraph pencil to draw the outline of the hole on the underside of the space mat.*

four *With a craft knife, cut a small circle from the centre of the outline and then make straight cuts from the inner to the outer circle.*

five *Apply PVA glue to the back of the chair and press the cut sections in place. Once the circle has been centred and the glue is tacky, apply the space blanket as a continuous strip.*

SHEER FABRIC CHAIR

A BEAUTIFUL CHAIR with wonderful curved legs, a ladder back and cane seat might not seem to need further treatment; yet sometimes, for a change, or for a special occasion, such as a wedding party or a Valentine's Day dinner, you might want to decorate a chair without masking its integral beauty. A wistful, romantic appeal can be given by swathing the chair in translucent fabric to give it a softness which looks very special. The transparent fabric could be coloured or use one of the metallic fabrics in gold or silver, so long as the bones of the chair show through. Tie the sash that takes up the extra fabric in a knot or a big, soft bow and leave it either at the back or on the seat, like a cushion.

YOU WILL NEED

wooden chair

tissue or pattern-cutting paper

pencil

dressmaker's pins

3m (3yd) of 137cm (54in) transparent silk, voile or organza

fabric marker

dressmaker's scissors

measuring tape

sewing machine, matching thread and iron

one *Trace the shape of the chair back rest. Use this as a template for cutting the back and front of the back rest co er, adding 2cm (¾in) all round for seams. Pin the template to the fabric, draw round it and cut out the pieces. Trace the shape of the seat in the same way. Transfer on to fabric, adding 2cm (¾in) for seams. Measure from the seat edge to the floor, for the depth of the skirt. Add 2cm (¾in) for seams.*

two *For the skirt, add 120cm (48in) to the circumference of the chair seat. Cut as one panel.*

three *For the sash, allow 2m (2yd) x 40cm (16in). Right sides facing, stitch the bottom of the front back rest panel to top of the seat panel.*

four *Press open all the seams as you go. With right sides together, stitch the front back rest panel to the back.*

five *Hem bottom of skirt. Press, pin pleats. Hem top of skirt. Sew to seat panel at sides and front and to back panel at back. Fold sash in half, right sides together. Sew seams. Turn right sides out, stitch open end. Tie to chair.*

FUN FUR CHROME CHAIR

ANOTHER COMMON junk-shop find is the chrome-framed chair. Suppliers of second-hand office furniture should have plenty of inexpensive examples. This one was in a very bad state when found – the chrome was spotted with rust and the padding torn. The finished picture shows how even a really tatty chair can be transformed into something smart. The fun-fur covering may seem a touch bizarre but, teamed with the chrome, it turns the chair into a real one-off. You need at least twice the length of each pad in fun fur.

YOU WILL NEED

chrome chair

screwdriver

chrome cleaner

soft cloth

craft knife

foam or wadding

staple gun

fun-fur fabric

one *Undo and reserve the screws and remove the old seat pads. Clean the chrome frame with chrome cleaner.*

two *Cut away the old covering fabric and padding, to reveal the wooden base of the pads.*

three *Cover the base and seat back with new foam or wadding, securing it with a staple gun. Replace the pads.*

four *Cover the pads with fun-fur fabric, using a staple gun to attach the fabric to the wood. Take into account the nap of the fabric, so it falls nicely over the curved edge. For the hardest wear, the pile should run from back to front (i.e. it lies flat when smoothed in that direction). Fold the fabric over the chrome supports. Replace the screws.*

POLYNESIAN THRONE

A SPLENDID ADDITION to your conservatory or log-cabin-style summer house, this chair festooned with wheat and rushes is not destined to be a mere garden seat, but a haven for sitting and musing. Gardening has become one of the most popular pastimes and garden centres are full of a huge variety of plants and garden paraphernalia. Customized garden furniture is much sought after and pricey, but you can make this stylish throne for very little, with dried grasses, craft brushes, raffia and twigs, which are available from garden centres or florists.

YOU WILL NEED

wooden chair
medium-grade sandpaper
oil-based brown paint
paintbrush
4 large bunches of wheat
large hank of raffia
double-sided tape
craft rush brushes
saw
staple gun
dried bamboo or rushes

one *Sand the wooden surfaces, to provide a key for the paint. Paint the chair with the brown paint to give it a wood-grain effect. You may find it easier to remove the seat.*

two *Cover the horizontal strut of the back rest with a few lengths of wheat, tying them in place with raffia. Use the double-sided tape to hold the wheat while you work (the final fixing comes later). Attach two rush brushes diagonally, by binding the stalks to the chair frame and at the crossing point with raffia. Shorten the two remaining rush brushes to the length of the vertical chair struts.*

three *To cover the verticals of the back rest, bind them with several strands of raffia. Slot stems of wheat through raffia until wood is covered. Tie the shortened brushes to the front horizontals and verticals.*

four *Bind the two side brushes with many twinings of raffia. Discreetly part the brushes and secure them at the top with a few strengthening staples. Add decorative and reinforcing raffia in crisscross fashion to the back of the chair. Knot the raffia to secure it.*

five *Choose thin, flexible bamboo or rushes to bend over the top of the legs, staple in place then bind with raffia. Staple a rough covering of wheat and rushes over legs. As a final touch, and also to help it last, knot and crisscross more raffia between your turns.*

BUCKET STOOL

FLORIST'S BUCKETS in galvanized tin are widely available in a variety of heights; obviously, the taller they are, the better. Cover the metal seat pad in any fabric (a waffle towel was used here). For a bathroom you could fill PVC or clear plastic fabric with foam chips or fun sponges. Tea towels also make fun covers and a layer of dried lavender would make a lovely scented seat.

YOU WILL NEED

1m (1yd) heavy cord or rope

2 florist's buckets

glue gun

very large self-cover buttons

scraps of material for covering buttons

fabric-cutting tool for buttons

waffle hand towel

circular cushion pad

large sewing needle

matching thread

one *Attach the cord or rope to the top rim of one of the buckets with the glue gun.*

two *Place this bucket inside the second bucket, applying glue to its rim, then invert both buckets.*

three *Use the fabric to cover the buttons as per the manufacturer's instructions. The special tool for cutting the fabric is invaluable for this job.*

four *Sew the buttons to the centre of the waffle hand towel. Then use the towel to cover the cushion pad. Instead of smoothing out the gathering in the fabric, accentuate it, using the buttons as a focus. Glue the pad to the upturned bucket.*

CARDBOARD CHAIR

IT'S VERY IMPORTANT that you hunt down the correct cardboard of the heaviest weight direct from a cardboard manufacturer for this chair. Here, a substantial "treble-skinned" cardboard has been used. The template shows how to make the chair by judicious folding. Remember that, as with wood, the vertical grain is the strongest. Cardboard furniture is particularly suitable for children, because of their lighter weight. To hold your cardboard creation securely together, use gum arabic tape, as it is a deceptively strong brown parcel tape and therefore perfect for this project.

YOU WILL NEED

felt-tipped pen

metal ruler

4 sheets of treble-skinned cardboard, 2 x 1.5m (2 x 1½yd)

scissors

craft knife

self-healing cutting mat

gum arabic tape

4 thin dowels, pencils or chopsticks, 13cm (5in)

one *Draw the design directly on to the cardboard, using the diagrams on the next page as a guide. Make sure that you keep the grain of the cardboard running from the top of the chair to the bottom.*

two *Using the back of a pair of scissors and the metal ruler, score along the fold lines and, using a craft knife, cut out all the shapes and bind the edges with gum arabic tape.*

three *Assemble the chair in the same way as you would make a carton, folding and slotting the cardboard into itself. The back rest of the chair has flaps that fold into the arm rests.*

four *Slot the seat into position, making sure it is securely held in place. To give further support on the struts, peg pieces of dowel, or even pencils or chopsticks, through the cross-struts.*

LOOSE CHAIR BACK

CHAIR SEAT

MAIN CHAIR
BACK AND SIDES

CONTINUED OVER ➤

LIGHT AND SHADE

Bent-Wire Chandelier ♦ *Angular Uplighter* ♦ *Pink Tissue Shade*

Eccentric Crepe ♦ *Bird Cage* ♦ *Chicken-Wire Torch*

Leading Lights ♦ *Handmade Paper Globe* ♦ *Raffia Standard*

Trimmed Shade ♦ *Trio of Lampshades* ♦ *Inca Bird Print*

Starry Night ♦ *Gilded Paper Patchwork* ♦ *A Shade Oriental*

Stained-Glass Bulb ♦ *Woody Nightshade*

INTRODUCTION

THE LIGHTING IN ANY ROOM IS CRUCIAL–it has a huge impact on the overall atmosphere. You can use it to highlight the contours of a room, to draw attention to desirable features and to tempt the eye away from less impressive corners. The options for interesting lights are endless, from high-tech spotlights to traditional standard lamps and classical sconces, and in this chapter we have tried to explore plenty of alternatives. Simple, step-by-step photographs show how to transform everyday lampshades and bases by using interesting paint techniques, by embellishing them with raffia or covering them with beads. You can take a basic frame and cover it with tissue paper, or wrap it with muslin, or create a table lamp from bamboo–all the projects we have chosen are clearly photographed for each project and provide a stunning gallery of different treatments for painting, adapting and decorating light fittings of all kinds. A good starting point is to look at the lights that are already in your home. Some of the quick projects could be just what is needed to give them an injection of style. Bases and shades can both be transformed with simple paint techniques or bead fringing, or stamped

*Left: The bird shapes stamped on to
this paper lampshade are inspired by
traditional Inca patterns.*

with paper designs. Patterns can be cut out of paper shades, to allow shards of light to escape and tin shades can be drilled or pierced for a similar effect. Old-fashioned wall lights that you no longer admire can be replaced with small spotlights and creatively shaded with unusual objects such as baskets, colanders, roof slates ... or perhaps you will come up with an unusual idea of your own. Lighting is more than a practical necessity, it is one of the interior designer's most powerful tools, so use it creatively and really enjoy transforming the look of your rooms.

Above: A pink paper lampshade is wonderfully frivolous and will cast a warm and comforting glow, just what you need as an antidote to the stresses of the world outside.

Below left: A light can in itself be an interesting object. Here, the conical shape complements decorative spears.

Below: Treat lampshades as blank canvases for your design ideas.

$\mathscr{B}$ENT-WIRE CHANDELIER

MAGICALLY CRAFTED FROM A roll of wire, this delicate little chandelier was twisted and curled into shape with long-nosed pliers. Making it is so much fun that you will probably want to make a pair. Bonsai-training wire, sold in garden centres and by bonsai-tree specialists, was used here. Hang the chandelier from a chain and hook so that it can twist and turn in passing air currents.

YOU WILL NEED

roll of silver bonsai-training wire

wire cutters

long-nosed pliers

roll of gardening wire

4 self-tapping screws and screwdriver

glue gun with all-purpose glue sticks

4 drawing pins

4 night-lights

large sequins

one *Cut a 35cm (13¾in) length of bonsai wire for the first kidney-shaped curl. Hold the wire with one hand, grip the end with the pliers and shape a curl. Holding the first curl in your hand, curl the other end. Make a single curl from a smaller piece of wire.*

two *Make two more single curls. Each branch is made of these four pieces. Cut a 12cm (4¾in) length of gardening wire and bind the kidney-shaped curl and two of the single curls together, as shown. Wind the wire round neatly like a spring.*

three *Screw a self-tapping screw into the centre of the binding, leaving at least 1cm (½in) protruding at the top.*

four *Bind the third single curl on to the back of the kidney shape, winding a length of gardening wire into a neat binding as before. Snip off the end of the gardening wire at an angle, close to the binding. Repeat the above steps to make the four branches.*

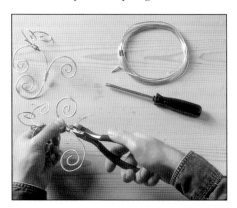

five *Cut a 50cm (20in) length of bonsai wire for the central column. Twist one end into a spiral and the other into a small hook. Make two small, tight curls and bind them into the top end of the column, facing inwards. Bind the four branches on to the column.*

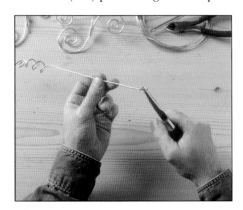

six *Apply a dot of glue to one of the screw heads and immediately sit a drawing pin on it, point upwards. Repeat with the three remaining screw heads. Press a night-light down on to each of the drawing pins. Thread the large sequins on to the curls.*

ANGULAR UPLIGHTER

THIS UNUSUAL WALL LIGHT IS a two-coloured plastic shade slotted over a standard mini-spotlight. The two halves of the shade are simply clamped together with two shiny sprung paper clips on each side. Before fitting the two pieces together, cut a hole in the back piece to slot over the base of the spotlight. Make the hole the same size as the spotlight base so that it fits snugly and will not slip. Fit the back of the shade in position first, making sure that the bulb will remain well clear of the plastic to avoid damage to the shade and any potential accidents.

YOU WILL NEED
brown parcel wrap
pencil
ruler and set square
scissors
spray adhesive
sheet of yellow plastic
sheet of red plastic
craft knife and cutting mat
small halogen wall-light
fixture
4 small sprung paper clips

one *Enlarge the template on a photocopier. Transfer it twice to brown parcel wrap. Cut out the two patterns, leaving a 2cm (¾in) seam allowance all around the edges.*

two *Spray the paper patterns with adhesive and stick one on each plastic sheet. Cut out the shapes and nick the ends of the fold lines, so that they will be obvious from both sides.*

three *Remove the paper, then score the fold line, but do not cut more than the surface as you do it. Practise on the off-cuts first to get the pressure right.*

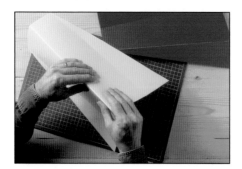

four *Turn the sheets over and score the fold lines again, working between the nicks at each end. Fold up the shades. Cut a hole in the back shade to fit the spotlight base, place it over the spotlight, then attach the front piece with paper clips.*

PINK TISSUE SHADE

THIS BRILLIANT PINK PAPER lampshade will make a stunning centrepiece for a room and will cast a flattering pink light over everything – and everyone – at the same time. Make the size of the lampshade appropriate for your room. As it is very lightweight, it can be made quite big, which is useful if your house has high ceilings. Attach equal lengths of chain to the curled hooks and hang the light fitting in the centre, so that the hot air rises out of the top of the shade.

YOU WILL NEED

bonsai-training wire

wire cutters

thinner wire

long-nosed pliers

chains to hang the shade

glue gun with all-purpose glue sticks

bright pink, good-quality tissue paper

water-based varnish

paintbrush

one *Cut three equal lengths of bonsai wire for the struts. Bend them into wavy shapes. You can exaggerate the shape as the wire will spring back a little. Bind the ends together with thinner wire, using long-nosed pliers.*

two *Attach a length of the thinner wire about 12cm (4¾in) from the end of one strut, winding it around to secure it. Then take it around the other two struts in the same way. This will form the top of the framework. Wind around two more lengths of the thinner wire in the same way.*

three *Using the pliers, curl the ends of the struts where the chains will be attached. Apply glue to one of the struts and fold the edge of a piece of tissue paper over it. Stretch the tissue across and glue it to the next strut.*

four *Continue in this way overlapping where necessary, until the framework is covered. Wind and glue a strip around the point where the three struts are joined. Brush on a coat of varnish to tighten up the paper and bond the layers.*

ECCENTRIC CREPE

CREPE BANDAGE IS GREAT material to work with and makes a fun lampshade. It has just enough stretch to give a good tight fit and the textured surface clings to itself as you layer the bandage. Keep an even tension as you wind it around a wire frame and use hot glue at key points, if necessary, to prevent any slipping or sagging. Make sure you leave an opening at the top, however, to allow the hot air to escape.

YOU WILL NEED

copper bonsai-training wire

wire cutters

long-nosed pliers

thinner wire

glue gun with all-purpose glue sticks

rolls of bandage

one *Cut three equal lengths of bonsai-training wire and bend each into three curves, using the pliers. The wire will straighten up when you release it, so exaggerate the shapes as you bend them.*

two *Bind the three ends of the bonsai wire firmly together with the thinner wire. Be generous with the amount of wire because you need to make a solid fixture. Use the long-nosed pliers to help you to bind tightly.*

three *Run another length of wire between the three struts, winding it tightly around each strut, to form the lowest of three enclosing wires that will later provide the framework for the bandage binding.*

four *Wind round two more lengths of wire to complete the frame. Twist the ends of the struts into curved "feet".*

five *Glue the bandage to a strut about 5cm (2in) from the binding at the top. Wrap tightly to fix firmly. Wrap the bandage around the framework, pulling it to get the tension right. Apply glue whenever it crosses a strut.*

six *Wrap and glue a small length of bandage to cover the wire binding right at the top of the framework. Use the glue gun to seal the edge and be sure to leave a 5cm (2in) gap around the top in order for the heat to escape.*

BIRD CAGE

ALREADY DECORATIVE AND DESIGNED to hang at eye level, birdcages need little adaptation to turn them into unusual oriental-style shades. This charming little wooden cage was made in the Far East. However, judging by the spacing of the bars, it cannot have been intended for keeping a real bird. Look out for wooden or bamboo cages like this in gift shops, florist's or import stores and even junk shops and jumble sales (as long as they are in good condition). If necessary, adapt the steps to suit the shape of the cage. Hang the lampshade from a chain so that it can twist in passing air currents and use a low-watt bulb for safety.

YOU WILL NEED

small wooden or
bamboo birdcage

saw

wire cutters

tissue paper

pencil

scissors

ready-mixed wallpaper paste

paintbrush

pendant lamp fitting

one *Using a saw and a strong pair of wire cutters, cut away the struts that make up the base of the cage.*

two *Roll a sheet of tissue paper around the top section of the cage – here it is conical. Mark the shape in pencil.*

three *Cut out the shape. Apply wallpaper paste to the inside of the struts of the top section. Roll up the tissue paper then unfold it inside the cage, pressing it against the pasted struts to form a lining. Trim away any excess.*

four *Cut out a rectangle of tissue paper to line the rest of the cage. Paste the inside of the struts, then place the tissue paper inside the cage, as before. Allow to dry. Ask an electrician to attach the pendant lamp fitting and to wire it to a flex.*

CHICKEN-WIRE TORCH

THIS DRAMATIC SHADE WOULD look fabulous in an entrance hall or at the top of a staircase, especially if it is teamed with an interesting paint finish. The basic shape is a cone, but the character relies on the layers of chicken wire interwoven with silver solder and copper wire. Spirals of wire, creating an unusual textural patchwork, hold the ragged, torn paper in place. The shade is hooked over a small halogen wall spotlight by means of a slit cut into the wire mesh. The light picks up the colours of the silver solder and the copper wire, adding a further layer of brilliance on top of the greyish wire mesh, and shines through the different paper textures. The shade is very lightweight, but a coat of black emulsion applied to the base of the cone will add visual weight and create a feeling of substance and balance.

YOU WILL NEED

90 x 60cm (36 x 24in) chicken wire

long-nosed pliers

hammer

wire cutters

small halogen wall-light fixture

silver solder

copper wire

3 different, highly textured natural-weave papers

black emulsion paint

paintbrush

screw and screwdriver

one *Roll the chicken wire into a tube with a 16cm (6½in) diameter. Using the pliers, pinch and twist the cut edges to make a firm fixing at one end.*

two *Roll the tube into a cone shape, so that the unfixed end tapers down to a point. Pinch and twist the cut wire to hold the shape firm.*

three *Compress the narrow end of the chicken-wire shape by hammering it on a hard surface. The wire mesh will scrunch up into a fairly solid mass.*

four *Use the wire cutters to make a slit in the back of the cone. This should be large enough to fit over the base of the wall-light fixture and allow the cone to lie flat against the wall.*

five *Cut two 50cm (20in) lengths of solder and weave them in and out of the mesh. Follow the shape of the cone, spiralling the wire upwards.*

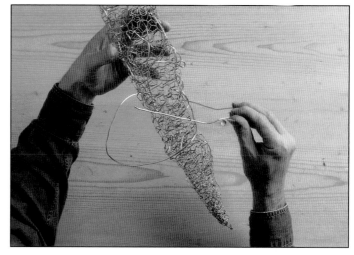

six *Cut similar lengths of copper wire and weave them through the mesh. Here a zig-zag pattern is used.*

seven *Wind copper wire around the outside of the cone, "sewing" it through the mesh in places.*

eight *Add a patchwork of chicken-wire pieces. The different depths of wire will be picked out and enhanced by the light when it is switched on.*

nine *Tear up the three sheets of paper. The edges should be rough and ragged. Tear some pieces into strips and others into random shapes.*

CONTINUED OVER ➤

ten *Place the paper pieces randomly on the outside of the cone, and use spiralling strands of wire to bind them into place.*

eleven *Use the long-nosed pliers to tweak and pinch the paper in places, so that it becomes a part of the structure instead of just sitting on the outside.*

twelve *Carefully dry-brush black emulsion paint on to the narrow base of the torch to give a matt-black charcoal finish.*

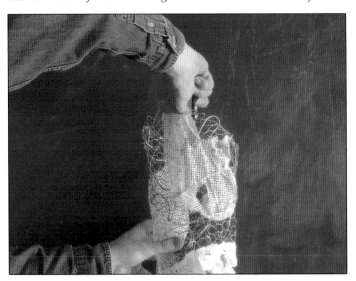

thirteen *Fit the torch over the wall-light fixture. Bend the mesh so that it fits snugly around the base and fix a screw in the wall near the top of the torch to hold it in place.*

Above: Chicken wire is cheap and surprisingly easy to work with. You can form the wire into elegant candleholders, candlesticks and shimmering bead domes.

LEADING LIGHTS

STRIKE A LIGHT! Change your shade and lamp base to something unique and quite sensational within the space of just an hour. Here, a basic shade was decorated with rough string threaded through punched holes. It is very easy to punch holes around the top and base of any shade, using a hole punch, and then thread through raffia, ribbon or wool. To continue this idea, put small string bows at intervals around the shade and intersperse them with dried leaves.

YOU WILL NEED
lamp base and shade
hole punch
rough string
scissors
glue gun and glue sticks
dried leaves

one *Punch evenly spaced holes around the top and bottom of the shade. Oversew lengths of string through the holes, top and bottom.*

two *Use the glue gun to stick the leaves around the shade.*

three *Tie small string bows and glue them between the leaves.*

four *Put a line of glue down the back of the metal base. Starting from the top, bind a long length of string tightly around the stem. Use a second length of string to cover the base. Press to make sure the string binding is absolutely firm. Make sure that the ends are glued securely in place.*

HANDMADE PAPER GLOBE

COVERING AN INFLATED BALLOON with papier mâché may not be the most original creative technique, but the old ideas are often the best ones. You could use a variety of different papers such as light tissue paper mixed with fibrous handmade-paper scraps, layering dried flowers and leaves between them. Keep the same thickness across the top of the balloon, but allow it to taper off towards the tied end.

YOU WILL NEED

inflated balloon

handmade paper scraps
containing leaves and
flower petals

ready-mixed wallpaper paste

paintbrush

cream or white tissue paper

gauze or mesh

pin

scissors

pendant lamp fitting

cardboard ring

all-purpose glue

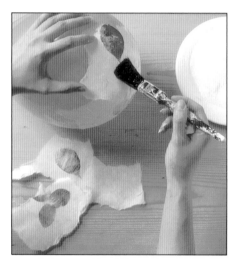

one *Apply paste to small pieces of paper and stick them on to the balloon in a random overlapping arrangement, beginning at the top.*

two *Cover the top two-thirds of the balloon with three layers of paper, tissue paper and gauze or mesh. Leave until bone-dry; this may take several days. Use a pin to burst the balloon and remove it from the shade.*

three *Cut a small hole in the top of the shade, using the light fitting as a guide to the right size.*

four *Reinforce the hole by gluing a cardboard ring inside the shade. Screw the two halves of the pendant lamp fitting together, one on either side of the shade, and ask an electrician to wire the fitting to a flex.*

RAFFIA STANDARD

STANDARD LAMPS PROVIDE the perfect overhead light to read by without killing the atmosphere of a room as bright central ceiling lights often do. Placing one in the corner means that an individual can see what he or she is doing, while the rest of the room can be dimmed for watching television or general relaxation. Here, a turned-wood standard lamp has been enclosed in a sheath of raffia that is finished off by a "thatched" base that resembles a very clean chimney-sweep's brush.

YOU WILL NEED
turned-wood standard lamp
rubber bands
several bunches of
natural-coloured raffia
scissors
coloured raffia

one *Place a rubber band at the bottom of the pole. Unravel the raffia and cut a handful of 38cm (15in) lengths. Fold the lengths in half and tuck them under the band, so that it holds them in place just below the fold. Continue inserting folded lengths until the base is completely covered.*

two *Wind a strand of raffia around the rubber band several times and tie it tightly to hold the raffia base in place.*

three *Place a rubber band around the top of the lamp. Tuck bunches of raffia under it until the pole is covered. About 25cm (10in) down from the band, wind a strand of raffia around the pole. Continue at intervals.*

four *At the base, tuck the raffia into the top of the base raffia, then bind to cover the join. Trim any loose ends. Cover the plain raffia bindings with coloured raffia.*

TRIMMED SHADE

TURN A RATHER BORING, plain-coloured lampshade into a completely wacky extrovert by adding a dangling fringe of unusual trimmings. Almost anything non-perishable that will thread can be used – the brighter, the better. The choice is yours. Check out the toyshop, especially the pocket money selection, where bright beads, miniature dolls and animals and fluorescent plastic balls are all waiting to be snapped up. Another good source is a stationery store; multicoloured plastic paper clips and treasury tags can be put to a decorative use their inventors would never have credited.

YOU WILL NEED

plain conical lampshade

square of paper or cardboard

pencil

set square

hole punch

strong thread

needle

selection of beads, toys, baubles, etc.

glue (optional)

one *Place the lampshade on a square of paper or cardboard and draw around the bottom edge in pencil.*

two *Use a set square to divide the circle into eight equal segments.*

three *Replace the shade on the paper or cardboard and mark the divisions around the edge in pencil.*

four *Use the hole punch to make eight small holes about 1cm (½in) up from the edge of the shade, in line with the pencil marks.*

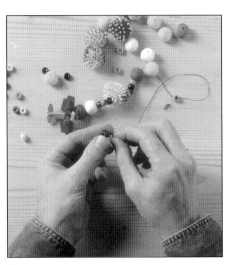

five *Attach a bead securely at the end of the length of thread, as an anchor, then thread on a selection of your chosen baubles and beads.*

six *Fix to the shade by sewing the thread through one of the punched holes several times, finishing with a secure knot. An extra bead can be glued to the edge of the shade to cover the thread. Decorate the rest of the shade in the same way.*

TRIO OF LAMPSHADES

NOTHING COULD BE QUICKER, easier or cheaper than painting squiggles, spots or flecks of colour on a few plain lampshades to add a touch of individuality to any room. The three shades shown here have each been made using a different decorative technique. All are fun to do, and only the black-and-white stripes require a steady hand. Use plain fabric shades and experiment with colour, using it to reinforce an existing decorating theme or to add a spark of brilliance and give a quick face-lift to a monotonous colour scheme.

YOU WILL NEED

BLOTTING-PAPER EFFECT
plain fabric lampshade
paintbrushes
bright blue ready-mixed watercolour paint
droppered bottle

PAINTED-LINE EFFECT
cardboard
cutting mat
plain fabric lampshade
scalpel
metal ruler
black acrylic paint
paintbrushes: large square-tipped and small

FLECKED EFFECT
plain fabric lampshade
cardboard
pencil
scalpel
cutting mat
toothbrush
water-based acrylic, poster, watercolour or gouache paints: yellow ochre, brick-red and cream
paintbrush

BLOTTING-PAPER EFFECT

one *Dampen the whole outer surface of the fabric lampshade with water, using a paintbrush.*

two *Fill the droppered bottle with blue paint and squeeze it gently to deposit one small drop on to the shade. Watch the blot spread so that you can judge where to position the next drop.*

three *Turn the lampshade with your free hand and, as you do so, drop equal amounts of paint, spaced fairly evenly all around the shade.*

four *Fill the spaces between the blots with a more random pattern of differently sized dots, but be careful not to cover all the original lampshade colour completely.*

five *Holding the lampshade from the inside with your free hand and resting your painting hand on the work surface, paint the top and bottom rims solid blue.*

PAINTED-LINE EFFECT

one *Cut a right-angled piece of cardboard with one edge the same length as the height of the shade. Angle the other side to make it easy to hold.*

two *Hold the square-edged cardboard up against the shade and paint a wide squiggle to the right of it, using the large brush. After each squiggle, move the cardboard along; this will ensure that you paint vertically and don't slide off in one direction, which is very easily done when painting a shape like this.*

three *Paint fine squiggly lines between the fatter ones, using the small paintbrush. Support the wrist of your painting hand with your free hand to keep it steady.*

four *Finish off the lampshade by painting the top and bottom rims with a solid black line.*

FLECKED EFFECT

one *Place the shade upside down on the piece of cardboard and draw around the inside of the top rim. Cut this circle out, just slightly larger than the drawn pencil line, and place it on top of the shade to prevent any paint from dripping on to the inside.*

two *Place the shade on a protected work surface. Fill the toothbrush with the yellow ochre paint, then draw your thumb backwards over the bristles to fleck the lampshade with colour. Try and get a fine, even covering, but allow the background to show through.*

three *Clean the toothbrush, then dip it into the brick-red paint. Use the brush at an angle, to make randomly placed wedge-shaped marks at different angles over the flecked pattern. Don't try for a regular pattern: look at the example shown here to judge the effect you are after.*

four *To finish the decoration, clean the toothbrush, then apply the cream paint in the same way as the red. It may not show up much but when the lamp is lit at night, all will be revealed.*

INCA BIRD PRINT

MAKE AN IMPRESSION on a tall conical lampshade by stamping it all over with a strong printed pattern. The shade used here is made of thin, mottled cardboard that resembles vellum in appearance and which casts a warm glow when the lamp is lit. The stamp is based on an Inca bird design that is bold enough for a beginner to cut and is even enhanced by a slightly rough cutting style.

YOU WILL NEED

white paper

spray adhesive

high-density foam

scalpel

PVA glue

flat plate

ready-made wallpaper paste

golden brown and darker brown ready-mixed watercolour paint in dropped bottle

small paint roller

conical paper lampshade

one *Photocopy the motif from this page. Spray the back of the copy lightly with adhesive and stick it on to the foam block. Cut around the shape with the scalpel and scoop away the back-ground so that the motif stands proud.*

two *Put about a dessertspoonful of PVA glue on to the plate. Add a similar amount of wallpaper paste and a few drops of golden brown paint and mix well. Run the roller through the mixture to coat it evenly and use it to coat the stamp.*

three *Print the bird motif on the lampshade by pressing the stamp on to the surface and then removing it directly. The wallpaper paste makes the paint gelatinous, leaving an interesting texture when you lift the stamp.*

four *Add a few drops of the darker paint to the mixture and stamp more motifs on the shade.*

STARRY NIGHT

CAPTURE A SMALL PIECE of the midnight sky by making this cut-out lampshade. Choose the deepest of blue shades, as the effect will be best if the light is completely blocked except by the star-shaped holes. The stars should be 1–2cm (½–¾in) wide; any smaller or larger and the effect will be lost. Use a very sharp scalpel to cut the points of the stars, and always cut from the top of a point towards the middle. The lampshade looks spectacular at night, but you will get a similar effect by day with the decoration of raised metal stars. Available from haberdashery stores, these have spikes at the back that are pressed through the shade and folded flat on the inside.

YOU WILL NEED

white paper

pencil

scissors

spray adhesive

navy blue paper lampshade

cutting mat

scalpel

metal star studs

high-density foam

one *Using the template, draw 50 stars on to white paper. Cut the paper into small squares with one star in the centre of each. Lightly spray the backs of the squares with adhesive and stick them inside the shade. Arrange them randomly rather than spacing them regularly or in a pattern.*

two *Rest the shade on the cutting mat, and cut out the stars using a scalpel. Working from the right side of the shade, cut through any threads that remain and gently push the stars inwards to remove them.*

three *Make sure that the spikes on the backs of the metal stars are all straight, otherwise they will not penetrate the shade. Hold a piece of dense foam inside the shade to give you something to push against, then press the stars through and fold the spikes over at the back.*

GILDED PAPER PATCHWORK

GIVE TWO PLAIN LAMPSHADES a glittering new look by covering them in paper patchwork in two different styles. Although the techniques for each shade differ slightly, they have enough in common to be used as a stunning pair. The paper can be any type that is not too thick: newsprint, tissue paper, parcel wrap, photocopied typescript, sheet music or fine woven papers. Make a feature of ragged edges and avoid a regular, neat finish. The very special linking finishing touch is added with flashes of brilliant gold. The leaf used here is called Dutch metal. It is applied in the same way as gold leaf but costs much less. If you have never done any gilding before, these shades are a good starting point.

YOU WILL NEED

CUT-PAPER PATCHWORK

selection of interesting paper materials: corrugated cardboard, coloured scrim ribbon, parcel wrap, handmade papers, paper mesh

scissors

plain cream fabric or paper lampshade

ready-made wallpaper paste or PVA glue

household paintbrushes for applying glue, an artist's paintbrush and a firm-bristled brush

gold size

Dutch metal leaf

soft cloth

TORN-PAPER PATCHWORK

selection of interesting paper materials: photocopied typescript, paper mesh, parcel wrap, handmade fibre paper, handmade paper, tracing paper

shellac (button polish)

household paintbrushes for applying stainers and glue, and an artist's paintbrush

methylated spirits

water-based stain: a natural wood shade

plain cream paper lampshade

ready-made wallpaper paste or PVA glue

gold size

Dutch metal leaf

soft cloth

CUT-PAPER PATCHWORK

one *Cut out "squares" from the different materials. Make them roughly equally sized, but trim them at an angle on both sides to taper slightly to fit the shade's conical shape.*

two *Try out various combinations of texture and colour until you are happy with the arrangement. Apply a coat of wallpaper paste or PVA glue to the backs of the shapes and stick them in place on the shade. Butt them against each other to form a solid patchwork.*

three *Paint "stitches" of gold size to link the squares together. Think of patchwork stitching, and make the lines vertical on the top and bottom and horizontal on the sides.*

four *Cut the Dutch metal leaf into strips, still on the backing sheet. Gently press the leaf on to the tacky gold size.*

five *Use a firm-bristled brush to clean away all the excess leaf, leaving just the stitches. Burnish with a soft cloth.*

TORN-PAPER PATCHWORK

one *Tear the different papers into similarly sized shapes, leaving the edges ragged and uneven.*

two *Tint one-third of the shapes with shellac. It is fast-drying and will make the papers stiffer and also slightly transparent. The brush will need cleaning with methylated spirits.*

three *Tint another third of the paper shapes using water-based stain and leave them to dry.*

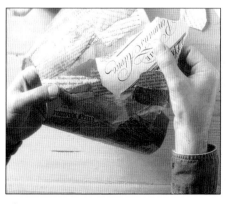

four *Arrange the shapes on the shade, overlapping them in places and making a feature of the ragged edges. Practise with different arrangements until you are happy with the result.*

five *Apply wallpaper paste or PVA glue to the backs of the shapes and stick them on to the shade, using the stained shapes first. Space them wide apart to start and build up gradually.*

six *Fill in the gaps with the untinted torn papers.*

CONTINUED OVER ➤

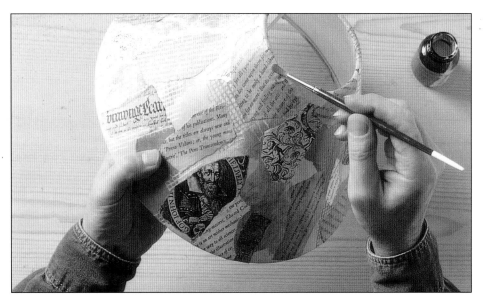

seven *Paint a neat 1cm (½in) border line all around the top and bottom of the lampshade with gold size.*

eight *Cut the sheets of Dutch metal leaf into strips, leaving the backing sheet still in place.*

nine *Press the strips against the tacky gold size along both edges. Overlap them when you need to; the leaf will only stick to the sized sections.*

ten *Finally, rub off any excess metal leaf and burnish the entire design to a shine with a soft cloth.*

A SHADE ORIENTAL

THE GLOBAL SUPERMARKET is now well and truly a part of our lives, and strings of brightly coloured fabric birds from the orient have become as familiar to us as imports from closer to home. The lampshade made here is a combination of Chinese bamboo weaving and Indian textile work, put together in a way that is reminiscent of an Australian bush hat! The lampshade looks best when hung low over a kitchen table or anywhere that needs light combined with vibrant colour.

YOU WILL NEED

string of Indian hanging textile birds

scissors

needle

embroidery thread

assorted beads

bamboo lampshade

scrap-paper measuring strip

one *Cut the retaining bead off the string of hanging birds, and remove the cord to separate the birds and beads.*

two *Thread the needle with about 30cm (12in) of embroidery thread and tie a bead at the end of the thread. Push the needle up through the existing hole in one of the birds, and then thread on three more beads.*

three *Attach the bird to the shade, allowing it to hang down three finger-widths from the rim. Divide the rim into ten equal sections and attach a bird at each division.*

four *Attach an inner row of birds one-third of the way up the shade. Position them so that they hang between the birds on the outer row and at a slightly higher level. Use a paper measuring strip to calculate the thread lengths required.*

STAINED-GLASS BULB

LIGHT BULBS CAN BE PAINTED in jewel-like colours to look like little illuminated stained-glass balls and create an unusual and impressive talking point. Ordinary light bulbs can be used, but the one shown here is a large 60-watt decorative globe bulb. Painted bulbs deserve to be shown off, so hang them low over a table, with a shallow shade that will not distract attention from the pretty patterns cast by the coloured shapes. Special glass paints are available from art and craft shops. You don't need to buy much, as a little paint will go a long way.

YOU WILL NEED
waterproof marker pen
3 pieces of cardboard
light bulb
scalpel and cutting mat
strip of cardboard
sticky tape
glass paints: pink, green, yellow, blue and black
paintbrushes

one *Draw a circle on each piece of cardboard: one the size of the widest part of the bulb, one the size of the centre of the star design and the third in between the two. Cut out the circles. Slip each piece of cardboard in turn over the bulb and draw a guideline on the glass where each sits. Carefully draw the guidelines for the rest of the design.*

two *Roll up the corrugated card strip to make a base for supporting the bulb. Secure the roll with sticky tape.*

three *Begin painting the top of the bulb. Start with the central dot and radiating arms of the star. Support your painting hand with your free hand to steady it.*

four *Working carefully, fill in all the different parts of the design, applying more than one coat where necessary to build up the colour. Allow the paint to dry, then paint a thick black line around each colour section to give a stained-glass effect.*

WOODY NIGHTSHADE

WOOD VENEER IS A THIN SHEET shaved from a seasoned tree trunk and is sold by timber merchants who supply furniture makers. Each sheet is unique, so choose the veneer with the best grain; it will look even better with light shining through it. The lampshade shown here is made from flamed-ash veneer. The veneer hangs from a simple wooden frame but you could use a square picture frame (without the glass). Carefully remove one edge of the frame, thread on the curtain rings and glue the piece back. Suspend the veneer from the frame using clipped curtain rings. Hang the lampshade on leather thongs or cord from a ceiling hook, with a pendant lamp fitting and bulb dangling inside it.

YOU WILL NEED

4 equal lengths of wooden dowel, mitred

glue gun with all-purpose glue sticks

curtain rings with clip attachments

metal ruler

scalpel

sheet of wood veneer

4 equal lengths of cord or leather thongs

one *Join three pieces of dowel using the glue gun. Thread the rings on to the frame before glueing the last piece of dowel in place.*

two *Measure the width of one side of the frame and, using the scalpel, cut four strips of veneer, one for each side. Make the length roughly twice the width; for a natural look the pieces should not be precisely the same size.*

three *To finish, attach two clips to each sheet of veneer, then tie a cord or thong to each corner for hanging.*

CONTAINERS

String Bottles ♦ Fanciful Shoe Box ♦ Blanket Chest

Button Box ♦ Star Cupboard ♦ Lizard-Skin Boxes

Moses Basket ♦ Pretty Pots ♦ All Boxed Up

Origami Boxes ♦ All the Trimmings ♦ News on Shoes

Gilded Boxes ♦ Punched Metal Bucket ♦ Circular Painted Boxes

Camembert Numbers ♦ Snowflake Storage Jars

INTRODUCTION

CONTAINER DECORATING PROVIDES highly imaginative and innovative projects for transforming old containers or creating new ones in quick, simple, stylish and beautiful ways. Put an end to cluttered shelves and overcrowded wardrobes, protect your belongings from dust, spillages or breakages and find exciting ways to jazz up your home. If you've always thought of containers as mere practical objects in which to store anything from flowers to biscuits, then you will be amazed at how cheap, everyday items can be easily made over into chic containers, bringing a personal dash of style into every room in your house. Take old paint tins, jam jars, bottles, bags, baskets or shoe boxes and give them a whole new lease of life by converting them into plant pots, shoe racks or funky chests of drawers - cover them with fabric, perhaps, or glue on buttons, beads or shells ... there are no limits to what you can do. The projects we show you can serve as a rich source of ideas to help you add a variety of colours, textures, patterns and shapes to whatever style of

Below: Choose containers with interesting shapes, such as the bottles pictured, then all you need to do is to emphasize their basic forms by adding texture to surfaces.

organization you opt for. Whichever
project you choose to make, you can
simply use our suggestions as a springboard
for your own creativity, so don't be afraid to amend or
embellish once your confidence has grown. Adapt ideas and
techniques to suit your own style and existing decor. An afternoon spent
sticking and gluing is totally absorbing and at the end of the day you will
have a wonderful sense of achievement, too. All the techniques used
here are clearly photographed for each project and are designed to be
easy to follow. Throw inhibition to the wind and enjoy creating great-
looking effects at next to no cost!

*Above: Favourite footwear deserves
the very best of care, so fashion a suitably stylish resting place.*

*Below left: Gilded boxes are easy to
make but create a luxurious mood.*

*Below right: Make paper boxes to fit
any size using origami techniques.*

STRING BOTTLES

LIQUEUR BOTTLES HAVE SUCH lovely shapes that it seems a shame to put them into the recycling bin. This method of recycling enables you to keep on enjoying them even after you have enjoyed their contents! The bottles used here are sherry, crème de menthe and Armagnac. This project is very easy to do and it can almost seem like therapy once you've gathered together a ball of string, some glue, a pair of scissors and three interestingly shaped bottles. Make yourself comfortable, put on some relaxing music and start winding the string round the bottles.

YOU WILL NEED

ball of string

glue gun with all-purpose glue sticks (or all-purpose glue)

3 interestingly shaped bottles

scissors

one *Coil one end of the string round like a drinks mat to make a base. Place a dot of glue in the centre of the bottle base. Heat the glue gun and apply glue in spokes over the base. Press the string on to them. Draw a ring of glue round the edge to make the base secure.*

two *Circle the bottle with the string, working your way up and applying sufficient glue as you go. Make sure you get a good bonding on the bends and curves.*

three *When you reach the top of the bottle, cut the end of the string and apply plenty of glue to it so the finish is neat with no fraying. Repeat these steps with the other bottles.*

FANCIFUL SHOE BOX

IF YOU ARE ONE of those people who always takes the shoe box home with new shoes, only to throw it away reluctantly a while later, then this is the project for you! Your instincts to take the box in the first place are right, as shoe boxes are the perfect shape and size to make useful containers. This box was covered with brown parcel wrap – yet more good recycling – that was rolled and twisted, then unravelled and stuck on to the box to provide an interesting textured surface. The "bark" is made from torn strips of white paper, coated with wood stain to give a streaky finish. The end result is a unique, natural-looking container suitable for anything from pot-pourri to a card index system.

YOU WILL NEED

shoe box

cream emulsion paint

paintbrushes

brown parcel wrap

pre-mixed wallpaper paste, and cheap brush

scissors

PVA glue

thick white paper

wood stain (such as antique pine)

thick, coarse string

piece of calico, 10 x 10cm (4 x 4in)

bulldog clips (or pegs)

glue gun with all-purpose glue sticks (or all-purpose glue)

one *Paint the shoe box with cream paint until all of the lettering is completely covered. Leave to dry.*

two *Roll up some parcel wrap, crumpling it. Fold up, then twist it as small as possible. Untwist and open out paper.*

three *Apply a coat of wallpaper paste to the box. Place it centrally on the parcel wrap.*

four *Fold the parcel wrap round the box, pressing it into the pasted surface, but not smoothing it too much. Pinch the paper along the edges of the box and cut along these. Fold the end flaps inside, sticking them in place with wallpaper paste.*

five *Fold the parcel wrap round the sides of the box, one end at a time, pasting one on top of the other to create two large triangular shapes.*

six *Fold the triangular shapes up over the sides and paste them against the inside of the box.*

seven *Neaten the inside by cutting a piece of parcel wrap to fit the base exactly. Paste it over the paper edges.*

eight *Using a dry brush, paint a streaky coat of undiluted PVA glue on the white paper. Leave some areas of the paper unpainted, to allow the wood stain to show through. Leave to dry completely.*

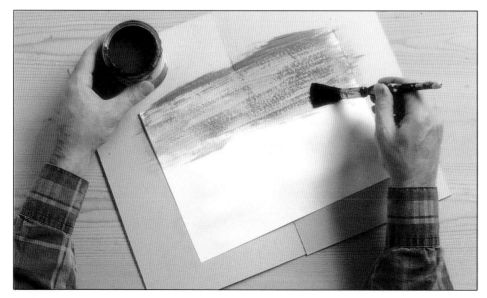

nine *Brush wood stain on to the white paper. It will be resisted by the PVA glue where it is at its thickest and part-resisted in other places. This gives the bark effect.*

ten *Tear the paper into rough triangular shapes. If you tear at a slight angle, the paper will rip through its thickness and make the edges white and thin. Paint these white edges with wood stain so that they blend in.*

CONTINUED OVER ➤

eleven *Roll up the paper triangles, beginning with the widest part and rolling towards the point. Bundle the strips together with string and tie a reef knot. Separate the strands of string so that they bush out from the knot.*

twelve *Fray the edges of the calico piece, then scrunch it up in the middle, using clips to hold the shape. Heat the glue gun and apply glue to the scrunched folds. Press the calico on to the centre of the box lid.*

thirteen *Remove the clips from the calico and apply more hot glue. Press the bark bundle on top of the calico.*

fourteen *If you are using the box to store a card index, write labelling on some spare "bark" paper and glue this to one end of the box.*

BLANKET CHEST

YOU CAN ALMOST GUARANTEE that every interesting pine chest has been discovered by now, stripped and sold for a profit, but there are still plain, solid work chests around which can be used as a good base for this project. The blanket used for covering the chest is the utilitarian sort used by furniture removal firms as a protective wrapping. Any blanket would be suitable, but this sort has lots of "give" because of the way it is woven and so can be stretched for a smooth fit. The chest has a piece of upholstery foam on it so it doubles up as a comfortable bedroom seat. The lid is held down by a leather strap – suitcase straps or old horse tack are ideal as they come in longer lengths than leather belts.

YOU WILL NEED
wooden chest
screwdriver
pliers
tape measure
blanket
dressmaker's scissors
staple gun
upholstery foam, to fit lid
ruler
cutting board
craft knife
upholstery tacks
scrap card
small hammer
piece of leather (or card)
leather strap

one *Unscrew and remove the hinges from the lid and remove any protruding nails or screws. Measure around the chest for the length of the blanket. Then measure the height of the chest. Double the height and add 13cm (5in).*

two *Cut the blanket to size. Spread it out, and lie the chest on its side in the middle with an even amount of blanket either side and 8cm (3in) below the base. Cut from the front edge of the blanket, in a straight line, to the left and right front corners of the chest. Staple the cut section inside the chest.*

three *Smooth the blanket down the side and staple it under the base. Cover the rest of the chest in the same way. Fold the blanket round from both sides to meet at the back, and staple it in place. Staple all the lining neatly inside.*

four *Cut a piece of blanket about 10cm (4in) larger than the lid on all sides. Place the foam in the middle of the blanket with the wooden lid on top. Press down the foam, pull up the blanket on one side and staple it in place.*

five *Cut a triangular section off each corner. Leave enough blanket to fold up and staple to the lid. Fold the cut edge up and staple it across the corner.*

six *Staple the side pieces over the first. Neaten by folding and trimming. Work on diagonal corners alternately.*

seven *Trim the chest and secure the fastening strap to the lower half with upholstery tacks. Use a card strip as a guide to keep the spacing even.*

BUTTON BOX

BUTTON BOXES are an old-fashioned delight that should not be allowed to disappear altogether. There was a time when most homes had a biscuit tin filled with an assortment of buttons for sewing and knitting projects. You can make your own button box to store these little treasures. The wooden box used here is an empty tea container with a sliding lid, covered with black felt and decorated with buttons.

YOU WILL NEED

wooden box with sliding or hinged lid

black emulsion paint

paintbrush

black felt

chalk

dressmaker's scissors

rubber-based fabric glue

craft knife

cutting board

buttons

glue gun with all-purpose glue sticks
(or all-purpose glue)

one *Paint the box black inside and out. Leave to dry. Then put it on the felt and draw the shapes needed to cover it in chalk: a rectangle for the base and long sides up to the grooves for the lid; a strip to cover the two ends and the base a second time; and a strip for the lid, stopping short of the runners.*

two *Cut out the felt pieces. Then spread fabric glue on to the base and sides of the box and smooth the shorter strip of felt on to it. The felt will stretch a bit at this stage. Spread a thin strip of fabric glue along the top edge of the sides and fold the felt over it. Leave to it to dry completely.*

three *Trim off any edges for a neat finish. Glue the longer strip of felt on to the base and up both of the ends in the same way. Trim off any excess. Cover the lid with felt, then begin arranging the buttons to make an attractive design.*

four *When you are happy with the design, use the glue gun to stick the buttons in place. The glue will set straight away, so work quickly and place the buttons accurately. Decorate the sides of the box with stripes of coloured buttons.*

five *Glue a row of white and pearl buttons along the top edge of the sides to complete the design.*

STAR CUPBOARD

THIS ATTRACTIVE LITTLE cupboard fits in the moment you have finished it. While its style is individual, it does not scream out for attention, and it has that comfortable, lived in look. It was painted, stamped, then painted again and finally, it was given a coat of antiquing varnish and rubbed back with a cloth in places. It glows from all the attention and took just one afternoon to make. This style of decoration is so simple that you might consider transforming other furniture in the same way.

YOU WILL NEED

wooden cupboard

emulsion paint (olive-green, off-white and vermilion)

paintbrushes

scalpel

kitchen sponge

PVA glue

matt varnish (antique pine)

kitchen cloth

one *Paint the cupboard with a coat of olive-green emulsion. While the paint is drying, use the scalpel to cut the foam into a star shape.*

two *Pour some off-white emulsion on to a plate. Dip a sponge star into the paint and print stars all over the cupboard. Leave to dry.*

three *Make a mixture of two-thirds vermilion paint and one-third PVA glue and coat the cupboard liberally.*

four *Finish with a coat of tinted varnish, then use a cloth to rub some off each of the stars.*

LIZARD-SKIN BOXES

THESE SMART ANGULAR BOXES look crisp and exclusive, but they are, in fact, no more than paper-covered foam board! They make great containers for jewellery, hair-slides or cufflinks and they would add a touch of elegance to any desk or dressing table. When you make your own boxes, there are no manufacturing constraints, so you can make them any shape you like, however unconventional. Foam board is light and easy to cut and stick. Buy it from art and craft suppliers, and buy lizard-skin paper from specialist paper shops.

YOU WILL NEED

foam board

cutting board

felt-tipped marker pen

ruler

craft knife

glue gun with all-purpose glue sticks (or all-purpose glue)

3 different lizard-skin papers

1 spray adhesive

one *Place the foam board on a cutting board and mark a four-sided angular shape for the base. Cut out the shape. Measure each side, then decide on the height of your box. Cut out four rectangular side sections to fit those measurements. Heat the glue gun and run a thin strip of glue along each base edge, then stick the sides on. The glue will set straight away, so work quickly and accurately.*

two *Place the box on a sheet of foam board and draw round it. Add 3–4cm (1¼–1½in) all round for the lid overlap. Cut this out. Do this again, taking off 1cm (½in) all round, for the lower half of the lid. Glue the two lid sections together. Cut a strip of lizard-skin paper wide enough to line the inside and outside of the box and to fold underneath. Apply spray adhesive to the paper, then wrap it round the box.*

three *Cut down into the corners and fold the paper inside the box. Do the same underneath, smoothing the paper flat on to the box. Apply more glue where necessary.*

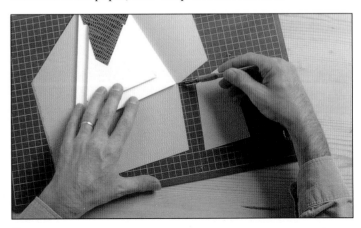

four *Cut out paper to cover lid. Glue in place and cut corners. Cut two identical shapes for a handle and glue together. Cover the handle with paper and glue to the top of the box.*

MOSES BASKET

THESE GENEROUS-SIZED WOVEN BASKETS were originally designed as easy, convenient and comfortable transport for young babies. Sadly, these old-fashioned cradles do not conform to stringent modern safety regulations, so present-day newborns have safer, but rather less charming, plastic and metal contraptions instead. Moses baskets are not completely redundant, however. They are used here as fresh and airy hanging containers for clothes and also provide an attractive decorative feature for a bathroom or bedroom. Alternatively you could use them for easy toy storage in a child's nursery.

YOU WILL NEED

plank of wood

tape measure

saw

sandpaper

drill, with wood and masonry bits

1 long or 2 short branches (or poles)

penknife (or wood carving knife)

dowel (optional)

2 Moses baskets

wood glue

hammer

wallplugs and screws

screwdriver

one *Cut two squares of wood at least 12 x 12cm (4¾ x 4¾in) and 5cm (2in) deep. Sandpaper the edges and drill a hole through the middle of each square, slightly smaller than the diameter of the branches. Carve away the branch ends so that they fit tightly into the holes. Sandpaper them slightly.*

three *Measure the distance across the basket, between the basket handles, and drill two holes the same distance apart on top of each branch. Apply wood glue to each branch and tap them into each square.*

two *Use dowels or offcuts from the branches for the pegs. Taper the ends.*

four *Apply wood glue to the peg ends and fit them into each branch. To fix the top branch to the wall, drill holes in the four corners of the square of wood, and four corresponding holes in the wall. Using the wallplugs and screws, screw the branch to the wall. Fix the lower branch to the wall allowing about 10cm (4in) clearance between the two baskets.*

PRETTY POTS

MINIATURE TOPIARY WILL LOOK both eye-catching and charming on a windowsill or collected together on a table, but don't forget to make the most of their containers. Terracotta pots have their own special appeal, but can also be treated to a variety of embellishments, from tassels to tape. Subtle, natural colours are best as they tone with the pots themselves and with the small pebbles used to conceal the florist's foam.

YOU WILL NEED

florist's dry foam block

sharp knife

3 old terracotta pots

2 straight twigs

glue gun and glue sticks

2 florist's dry foam balls

fresh foliage, such as box or privet

selection of pebbles

curtain weight

fine string

string tassels

masking tape

craft knife

self-healing cutting mat

matt varnish

paintbrush

one *Cut the florist's foam blocks in half and cut each block to fit into the pots. Position the foam in the pots. Insert the twigs and then glue them in place, to act as the stems of the trees. Glue the foam balls on top.*

two *Cut small pieces of foliage to the required size and insert them at random in the foam balls, to create a casual, carefree effect.*

three *Cover the foam in the pots with a layer of small pebbles so that it is completely concealed.*

four *Thread the curtain weight on to string and tie it around one of the pots. Decorate the other pots with tassels or designs cut from masking tape with a craft knife. Varnish to make the masking tape secure.*

ALL BOXED UP

THERE IS A HUGE VARIETY of boxes available, ranging from plain and simple white wooden boxes via shoe boxes to oval trinket boxes. Make a toning set of three using easily available natural materials. However, boxes can be trimmed with almost anything you like: bottletops, paper clips, string, rope or a collage of stamps. Linen tape (used in upholstery or for tags) is available from haberdashery departments.

YOU WILL NEED
plain wooden box
tape measure
scissors
linen tape
needle
matching sewing thread
2 wooden beads or toggles
glue gun and glue sticks
larch twig
small slatted wooden box
small packet of pot-pourri
small Shaker-style box
dried leaves and fir cones

one *Measure the plain wooden box. Allow an extra 2cm (¾in) at one end for the toggle and about 7.5cm (3in) for the loop and tag. Cut two lengths of linen tape to this length. Sew a loop in the end of each tape and attach the wooden beads to be used as toggles.*

two *Secure the tape to one end of the box with glue, leaving the toggle and loop free so the lid can be opened. Repeat on the other side. Glue a larch twig to the top of the lid, as a decorative "handle".*

three *For the slatted wooden box, sort through the pot-pourri and choose the items you would like to use. Glue them to the lid. Glue the dried leaves and cones to the Shaker box, and glue linen tape around the sides.*

ORIGAMI BOXES

ORIGAMI IS THE JAPANESE ART of paper-folding where the most extraordinary three-dimensional objects are made from a single folded square of paper. This little box is a suitable project for a complete beginner, but it may take a couple of practice attempts before it suddenly "clicks". You can make the boxes any size you like, and use any paper that is not too flimsy. Parcel wrap is good as it creases well and is cheap and strong.

YOU WILL NEED

sheet of paper

scissors

double-sided tape
(this breaks all the rules!)

selection of paper squares
for practice (optional)

one *Fold and trim a sheet of paper to make a perfect square. Fold the square corner to corner. Open it to show the creases of four equal triangles. Turn it over and fold into four square quarters. Unfold it so you can see the creases of eight equal triangles. The centre of the paper is Point A.*

two *Hold the model in the air and push all the sides together so that the corners meet in the middle. Flatten the model. Point A is now a corner of the flattened model. Keep it facing you.*

three *Fold the point opposite Point A over to meet it. Crease it along the mid-line. Now fold it back up to the mid-line and crease the fold. Unfold it again. Fold the same point up to the last crease, then fold it over again, up to the mid-line. Turn the model over and repeat this step.*

four *With point A still facing you, take the top layer of the left-hand corner and fold it over on to the right-hand corner. You are now faced with a square. Fold the left-hand corner and the top layer of the right-hand corner into the centre point, and crease. Bring the right-hand top layer over on to the left. Turn over and repeat.*

five *Point A now forms the base of a smaller triangle. Fold this up at the point where it meets the sides. Crease, fold it in the other direction and crease. Unfold. Insert your hand and splay your fingers while pushing up the bottom of the model, Point A. Fold down the two pointed sides level with the others and tuck the ends under. Secure with a small piece of tape.*

ALL THE TRIMMINGS

CHOOSE THE CHEERFUL PRIMARY colours of blue and red and team them with white for a crisp, clean look with a slightly nautical feel. Equally, you can trim black with white for classic appeal or use toning colours for adding a subtle lift. Felt is an easy, lovely and inexpensive way to trim plain fabrics, whether on shoe bags, linen bags, throws or cushions. You can add as much or as little decoration as you choose.

YOU WILL NEED

round template

2 squares of red felt, about 20 x 20cm (8 x 8in)

2 squares of blue felt, about 20 x 20cm (8 x 8in)

dressmaker's pins

fabric marker

pinking shears

blue cord

string

needle

matching sewing thread

fabric item, such as a shoe bag or quilt

one *Find a round template: it could be a tin lid, coin or anything similar. Place the template on the felt, and draw round the template with a fabric marker. Cut around the circle with pinking shears.*

two *Pin two circles together, knot short lengths of cord and sew them on to the circles.*

three *Repeat with lengths of string. Sew the circles on to your shoe bag, quilt or other fabric items.*

NEWS ON SHOES

SPECIAL SHOES DESERVE a home of their own and these sturdy wooden wine boxes can be made stylish enough to house anything from country brogues to Cinderella's glass slippers. The boxes were lined with different types of newsprint, which was layered and stuck down like papier mâché. Select your newsprint to suit your shoes – put leather lace-ups in the pink financial pages, party shoes in comic strips and velvet pumps in the arts and literary review pages.

YOU WILL NEED

wooden wine crates
sandpaper
PVA glue
paintbrushes
variety of newsprint
craft knife
clear matt varnish
(or shellac button polish)

one *Sand down the wine crate. Then mix PVA glue with water (50:50) and apply a coat to the inside.*

two *Apply another coat of the PVA mixture, then smooth newsprint over the inside. Apply undiluted PVA along the top edges and smooth the paper over it. Leave to dry before applying more paper and glue at random.*

three *Leave to dry, then trim the paper along the outside top edges with a craft knife. Varnish the whole box with either clear matt varnish or, if you want an "aged" look, shellac. Leave to dry, then re-coat at least twice.*

GILDED BOXES

THERE IS NO PAINT OR SPRAY that gives a finish to compare with gold leaf, or its cheaper counterpart, Dutch metal leaf. It glows and glitters and can be burnished with a soft cloth to leave a gleaming surface. The art of gilding is surrounded by mystique because it requires a great deal of skill to lay the fragile sheets of gold leaf on to gold size or glue. This design was created using a kit suitable for beginners, which can be bought from art and craft suppliers. The flat surface of the box makes it easy to apply, but it is important to follow the manufacturer's instructions as the drying time is crucial to the success of the project.

YOU WILL NEED

design tracing or photocopy
spray adhesive
high-density foam
craft knife
round painted wooden box
with lid
fine-grade sandpaper
pencil
gold leaf kit
paintbrush
plate
small foam roller
cotton wadding
fine wire wool (optional)

one *Select a suitable design or motif from a source book, and photocopy or trace to size. Spray the back of the design with adhesive and stick it on to a block of foam.*

two *Carefully cut out the design, starting in the middle. Then cut around the outside.*

three *Once the cutting is complete, carefully peel off the paper pattern.*

four *Rub the entire surface of the painted box lightly with fine-grade sandpaper to make a rough surface for applying the gold size.*

six *Carefully paint a strip of gold size between the edge of the box lid and the pencil line.*

five *Draw a pencil line around the top edge of the lid. Use your fingers to keep the line an even distance from the edge.*

seven *Put some size on to a plate and run the roller through it until it is evenly coated. Using the roller, coat the foam stamp thoroughly and evenly.*

eight *Stamp an even pattern round the side of the box, re-coating the stamp after each print. Stamp four shapes inside the lid border line and one in the centre.*

ten *Holding the box at an angle, apply the sheets of gold leaf round the sides in the same way.*

nine *Leave the size until it has the right degree of "tack" (according to the manufacturer's instructions), then invert the lid on to a sheet of gold leaf. Smooth the gold leaf over the edges so that it is in contact with all of the size.*

CONTINUED OVER ➤

eleven *Rub the surface with cotton wadding. All the "un-sized" gold will flake off, leaving the design behind.*

twelve *If the brand new gleaming design overwhelms you, rub the box lightly with wire wool to create an antiqued look.*

PUNCHED METAL BUCKET

THE IDEA OF DECORATING metal objects with raised punched patterns has been around ever since sheet metal was invented about 300 years ago. Silver is probably best-known for this decorative treatment, but cheaper metals can also look very impressive. Bare metal buckets are ideal for this sort of pattern-making, and all you need is a pen to draw your guidelines and a hammer and blunt nail for the punching. You can practise your technique on any tin can to find the ideal sort of tap needed to make a good bump without piercing the metal.

YOU WILL NEED

bare metal bucket

felt-tipped marker pen
(not water-based)

blunt nail
(or centre punch)

hammer

rag

lighter fuel
(or similar solvent)

one *Draw your pattern on the inside of the bucket. These motifs come from South America, but any repeated curves or angles are suitable.*

two *Rest the bucket on a piece of wood to protect your work surface. Tap the nail with a hammer, keeping the dents regularly spaced. About 1cm (½in) is fine.*

three *Continue hammering the pattern all over the inside of the metal bucket.*

four *Use a rag and lighter fuel to clean off the marker pen pattern that is left between the punched marks.*

CIRCULAR PAINTED BOXES

THIS PROJECT EXPERIMENTS with three different paint effects. The first, rust, looks especially good when used on a material that doesn't naturally rust, such as wood. Verdigris is a natural substance that forms on the surface of weathered brass and is a beautiful turquoise-green colour. The third finish used here is crackle glaze (craquelure) which looks a bit like lizard skin. This is the most time-consuming of the three paint effects because of the drying time needed between coats.

YOU WILL NEED

3 wooden boxes, with lids

water-based paints: dark grey, 2 shades of rust, green-grey, stone, 2 shades of green and maize yellow (according to required finish)

handful of fine sand

plate

paintbrushes

3 foam sponges

clear matt varnish, craquelure base varnish, craquelure varnish

alizarin crimson oil paint

2 rags

white spirit

THE RUST FINISH

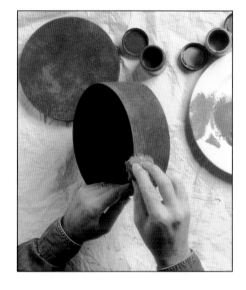

one *Mix sand into the dark grey base coat for texture. Apply two coats of paint to the box. Leave to dry. Dab on the darker rust colour with a sponge. Cover most of the background.*

two *Dab on the lighter rust colour. If you are in any doubt about how it should look, find some real rust and copy it. Finally dab in just a touch of green-grey. Do not overdo this as it should blend in rather than stand out as a sharp contrast.*

THE VERDIGRIS FINISH

Paint the box with the stone base coat colour. Dab on the lighter green with a sponge. Cover most of the background with this. Dab on the other green using a sponge. Apply a coat of clear matt varnish to protect the surface.

THE CRACKLE GLAZE FINISH

Paint a yellow base coat and a coat of craquelure base varnish. When dry, apply a coat of craquelure varnish. Leave to dry. Rub crimson oil paint into cracks with a rag. Dip a rag in white spirit; rub the surface so red paint remains in the cracks.

CAMEMBERT NUMBERS

THIS PROJECT SHOULD be linked to a wine and cheese party or the befriending of a French restaurateur as it involves nine Camembert boxes. It is always a relief to be able to recycle packaging and these empty boxes are certainly given a new lease of life in the form of a stylish set of containers. Enlarge the numbers on a photocopier so they fit your boxes and cut them out as stencils. If you find the task too daunting, trace the numbers on to the boxes and paint them in.

YOU WILL NEED

9 Camembert boxes

fine-grade sandpaper

clear matt acrylic varnish

paintbrushes: medium, stencilling, fine-pointed and square-tipped

number templates

craft knife

cutting board

spray adhesive

stencilling plastic or waxed stencil card

enamel paint: 9 colours plus silver

pair of compasses and pencil (optional)

shellac button polish

one *Remove any paper labels from the boxes. Rub the wood with sandpaper to get rid of any rough edges. Apply a coat of clear matt acrylic varnish to all the boxes.*

two *Take the templates or, to make your own, enlarge them on a photocopier so the numbers are 8cm (3in) high (or to fit within a border of about 1.5cm (⅝in). Cut each one out.*

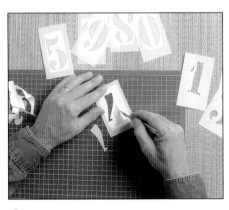

three *Stick the photocopies on to the stencil material with spray adhesive. Stick them underneath stencilling plastic, but on top of stencilling card. Cut out, making the incisions away from the corners.*

four *Stencil a number on each lid in different colours. With a fine-pointed brush paint a band about 1.5cm (⅝in) wide around each lid. (If necessary, use a pair of compasses). With a square-tipped brush, paint a band of silver around the edges. When dry, rub them down lightly and apply button polish.*

1 2
3 4
5 6
7 8
9 0

SNOWFLAKE STORAGE JARS

ALMOST EVERY KITCHEN COULD DO with a face-lift every now and then. Rather than pay over the odds for a completely new look, why not just cheer up your storage jars, simply and inexpensively, and give your kitchen a breath of fresh air? You can create a whole new atmosphere, and a really individual look, by stamping patterns on your jars with acrylic enamel paint. The finish is quite hard-wearing and is tough enough to stand up to occasional gentle washing, but take note that it will not withstand the dishwasher.

YOU WILL NEED
pencil
tracing paper
spray adhesive
upholstery foam
scalpel
kitchen cloth
glass storage jars
white acrylic enamel paint
plate
tile

one *Trace your chosen pattern shape, lightly spray it with adhesive and place it on the foam. Cut around the outline with a scalpel. Cut horizontally into the foam to meet the outline cuts and remove excess foam.*

two *Clean and dry the glass jars. Spread a coating of paint onto a plate and make a test print on to a tile to remove excess paint from the stamp.*

three *Holding the jar steady, press the foam around the side of the jar.*

four *Rotate the stamp 90 degrees and make the second print directly below the first. Continue in this way, alternating the angle of the print.*

INDEX

'African Days' 34-5
'All Boxed Up' 234-5
'All the Trimmings' 238-9
'Angular Uplighter' 174-5
'Animal Cushions' 112-13
'Artist's Studio' 38-41
'Astroturf Chair' 146-7

bags, shoe 238-9
basket, Moses 230-1
'Beach Mat Bed' 104-5
beach mat
  bed hangings 104-5
  blinds 36-7
bead curtains 48-9
bedheads 126-7
  renaissance 128-9
  tartan 126-7
beds 92-129
  adding colour 96-7
  beach-mat hangings 104-5
  bedheads 126-7 128-9
  canopied 102-3, 106-7
  cushions 98-9
  four-poster 104-5
  headboards 120-1, 122-3

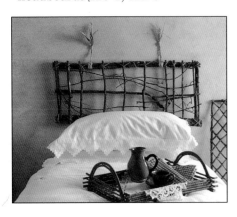

  lace-trimmed 100-1
  love pillows 116-7
  photocopied images 108-11
'Bent-Wire Chandelier' 172-3
'Bijou Boudoir' 20-3
'Bird Cage' 180-1
'Black and White Prints' 108-11
'Blanket Chest' 222-3
blankets, curtains 42-3

blinds
  beach mat 36-7
  insect 24-5
  windbreak 44-5
bottles, string-covered 216-17
boxes
  button-covered 224-5
  Camembert Numbers 250-1
  circular 248-9
  gilded 242-5
  lizard-skin 228-9
  origami 236-7
  sets 234-5
  shoe boxes 218-21, 240-1
broderie anglaise 96-7
'Brown Paper Panelling' 68-9
'Bucket Stool' 164-5
buckets, punched metal 246-7
'Button Box' 224-5
'Buttoned Blankets' 42-3

'Camembert Numbers' 250-1
'Canopied Bed' 102-3
canvas curtains 38-41
'Cardboard Chair' 164-7
chairs 130-67
  astroturf 146-7
  cardboard 164-7
  fabric swathed 144-5
  fake fur 158-9
  Nova suede 150-1
  special occasions 134-5
  translucent fabric 156-7
  vacuum-formed 154-5
  wheat and rush decoration 160-1
chandeliers
  bent-wire 172-3
  twig 52-3
'Checked Floor Mats' 80-1
chest, blanket covered 222-3
'Chicken-Wire Torch' 182-5
'Chintz Headboard' 120-1
chrome chair 158-9
'Circular Painted Boxes' 248-9
clips, curtain 14-15
'Coloured String' 60-1
conservatory chair 146-7

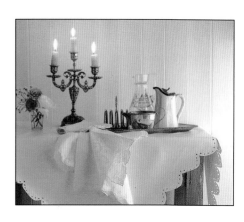

containers 212-53
'Cork-Stamped Floor' 70-1
cotton sheets, drapes from 10-11
crepe bandage lampshade 179-80
crystal drops, tie-backs 18-19
'Crystal Ties' 18-19
cupboard 226-7
'Curtain Call' 12-13
curtains 6-53
  bead 48-9
  canvas 38-41
  clips 14-15
  cotton sheets 10-11
  Kenyan cloths 34-5
  lace 28-9
  linking 26-7
  milliner's velvet 50-1
  muslin 14-15
  netting 20-3
  pot-pourri trimmings 12-13
  tartan rugs 46-7
  tie-backs 16-17, 18-19
  wall coverings 54-7
cushions, bedrooms 98-9, 112-13

drapes
  beds 102-3, 106-7
  cotton sheets 10-11
  lace 26-7
  muslin 14-15
  see also curtains
'Dream Trellis' 114-15
'Dressing for Dinner' 134-5

'Eccentric Crepe' 178-9
'Egyptian Dream' 10-11

'Egyptian Table-Top' 142-3
emergency blankets, chair covers 54-5
'Entwined Headboard' 122-3

'Fabric Swathed Chairs' 144-5
'Fabric Wall' 66-7
'Fake Animal-Skin Rug' 72-3
'Fanciful Shoe Box' 218-21
'Faux-Soapstone Floor' 74-7
floor mats, checked 80-1
floors 54-91
  cork-stamped 70-1
  faux-soapstone 74-7
  photocopy montage 82-3
  pop art 88-9
  rubber mats 78-9
  rug 72-3
  stencilled hardboard 84-7
  studded 90-1
flower pots 232-3
four-poster beds 104-5
'Fun Fur Chrome Chair' 158-9
fur, fake 72-3, 158-9

'Gilded Boxes' 242-5
'Gilded Paper Patchwork' 202-5
'Gingham Headboard' 118-9

halls, windows 24-5
'Hammock Quilt' 124-5
'Handmade Paper Globe' 188-9
'Hanging Around' 52-3
hangings
  twig 52-3
  wire 30-3
hardboard floor 84-7
headboards
  chintz 120-1
  entwined 122-3
  gingham 118-9
'Hula-Hula' 44-5

'Inca Bird Print' 198-9
insect blinds 24-5

jars, storage 252-3

Kenyan cloths, curtains 34-5
kitchens, windows 24-5
lace

bed linen 100-1
  curtains 28-9
lampshades 168-211
  bird cage 180-1
  chicken wire 182-5
  crepe bandage 178-9
  gilded paper patchwork 202-5
  oriental 206-7
  painted 194-7
  paper globe 188-9
  pink tissue 176-7
  stained glass 208-9
  stamped pattern 198-9
  star effects 200-1
  trimmings 192-3
  uplighter 174-5
  wood veneer 210-11
'Leading Lights' 186-7
lights 168-211
  chandeliers 172-3
  standard lamp 190-91
  uplighter 174-5
  see also lamps, lampshades
'Lizard-Skin Boxes' 228-9
loop-headed curtains,
  trimming 12-13
'Love Pillows' 116-17

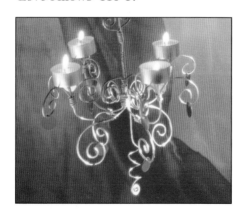

'Lovely Linens' 96-7

'Mad Hatter' 50-1
'Magic Beads' 48-9
'Magic Chair' 150-1
mats
  checked 80-1
  rubber 78-9
milliner's velvet curtains 50-1
montages, photocopy 82-3
'Moses Basket' 230-1
mosquito netting, beds 106-7

mouldings, chair 150-1
muslin
  bed drapes 102-3
  window drapes 14-15

napkins 140-1
netting
  beds 106-7
  curtains 20-3
'New Ways with Napkins' 140-1
'News on Shoes' 240-1
'No-Problem Links' 26-7
Nova suede, chair 152-3

'Origami Boxes' 236-7

'Panels and Stamp Motif' 62-3
paper
  brown 68-9
  lampshades 176-7, 188-9
  origami boxes 236-7
  wall hangings 58-9, 68-9
'Parchment Paper Art' 58-9
patchwork lampshade 202-5
photocopies
  bed linen 108-11
  floors 82-3
'Photocopy Montage' 82-3
pillows
  adding colour 96-7
  love 116-17
'Pink Tissue Shade' 176-7
'Polynesian Throne' 160-1
'Pop-Art Floor' 88-9
poster, bedhead 128-9
pot-pourri
  curtain trimmings 12-13
  table decoration 134-5
'Pretty Pots' 232-3

'Punched Metal Bucket' 246-7
'Punched Tin Wall' 64-5
'Pure Plastic' 136-7

quilt, hammocks 124-5

'Raffia Standard' 190-1
'Rainbows' 24-5
'Renaissance Headboard' 128-9
'Ribbons and Lace' 28-9
'Robinson Crusoe Blinds' 36-7
'Romantic Netting' 106-7
'Rope-Bound Chair' 150-1
rope decoration chair 150-1
  headboard 122-3
'Rubber Mats' 78-9
rugs
  bedhead 126-7
  fake fur 72-3
  window drapes 46-7

sari curtains 28-9
'Scotland the Brave' 46-7
'Shade Oriental' 206-7
'Sheer Fabric Chair' 156-7
sheets, adding colour 96-7
'Shell Tie-Backs' 16-17
shoes
  bags 238-9
  boxes 218-21, 240-1
'Snowflake Storage Jars' 252-3
'Space-Age Chairs' 154-5
'Stained-Glass Bulb' 208-9
staircases, windows 24-5
stamps
  floors 70-1
  lampshades 198-9

wall panels 62-3
standard lamp 190
'Star Cupboard' 226-7
'Starry Night' 200-1
'Stencilled Hardboard' 84-7
'Stool with Wood' 148-9
stool, bucket 162-3
storage jars 252-3
string
  bottle decoration 216-17
  wall hanging 60-1
'String Bottles' 216-17
'Studded Floor' 90-1

tablecloths
  plastic 136-7
  tactile 138-9
tables 130-43
  Egyptian motifs 142-3
  napkins 140-1
  special occasions 134-5
'Tactile Tablecloth' 138-39
'Tartan Bedhead' 126-7
tartan rugs
  bedhead 126-7
  curtains 46-7

terracotta pots 232-3
tie-backs
  shell 16-17
tin, punched 64-5
tissue lampshade 176-7
translucent fabrics, chair 156-7
trellis, headboards 14-7
'Trimmed Cushions' 98-9
'Trimmed Shade' 192-3
'Trio of Lampshades' 194-7
twig headboard 114-15

uplighter 176

velvet curtains 50-1
veneer lampshade 210-11
'Victorian Lace' 100-1

walls 54-69
  brown paper panels 68-9
  fabric coverings 54-7
  paper hangings 58-9
  punched tin designs 64-5
  stamp motif 62-3
  string 60-1
webbing, tablecloths
  140-1
'White Mischief' 14-15
windbreak blind 44-5
windows 6-53
  blinds 24-5, 36-7, 44-5
  hanging decorations 30-3, 52-3
  see also curtains
'Wired-Up Window' 30-3
wood mouldings, chairs 148-9
'Woody Nightshade' 210-11